STIR CRAZY IN KAZAKHSTAN

One person's experience, coping with living and working in a strange environment where normal, day to day activities can turn out to be monumental in their execution and where any comfort zones are hard to find!

KATY WARNER

authorHOUSE

AuthorHouse™ UK
1663 Liberty Drive
Bloomington, IN 47403 USA
www.authorhouse.co.uk
Phone: 0800.197.4150

© 2015 Katy Warner. All rights reserved.

No part of this book may be reproduced, stored in a retrieval system, or transmitted by any means without the written permission of the author.

Published by AuthorHouse 08/10/2015

ISBN: 978-1-5049-4425-0 (sc)
ISBN: 978-1-5049-4424-3 (hc)
ISBN: 978-1-5049-4426-7 (e)

Print information available on the last page.

Any people depicted in stock imagery provided by Thinkstock are models, and such images are being used for illustrative purposes only.
Certain stock imagery © Thinkstock.

This book is printed on acid-free paper.

Because of the dynamic nature of the Internet, any web addresses or links contained in this book may have changed since publication and may no longer be valid. The views expressed in this work are solely those of the author and do not necessarily reflect the views of the publisher, and the publisher hereby disclaims any responsibility for them.

Contents

1: The Decision and Leaving 1
2: Induction 4
3: Life Begins in Pavlodar 11
4: Locked Out – And In 14
5: A Trip to The Hospital 21
6: Another Shock 28
7: Lily From Vogue 31
8: Sharing Skills 35
9: More Frustrations and Light Relief 40
10: Interesting Excursions 46
11: A Very Strange Christmas 55
12: Time to Review 62
13: The Trip to Aktau 70
14: No Smoking Here 79
15: Back in The UK, Briefly 84
16: Return to Pavlodar 88
17: The Queen's Birthday 93
18: Misha's Problems Increase 100
19: The Wedding 108
20: Another Fall 112
21: Beginning of Endings 118
22: A Wonderful Trip 123
23: Final Days in Kazakhstan 130

One

The Decision and Leaving

I was here, locked in a strange flat, God knows where, with nothing to do, no-one to speak to, no clean clothes and no toothbrush. This was not a nightmare. Unfortunately it was reality. I entertained myself by practising my yoga, practising my Russian and writing in my diary. Before I retired to bed – early, very early – I took a shower, only to find as much water spilled out from the tap and onto the floor as came through the hose. Fortunately the towels and bedding were all new as Vadim had only just moved in, though he was not here now.

I awoke the next morning around 8.30 a.m. to hear dogs barking, cocks crowing and chickens squawking. I was still locked in, with nothing to do, no one to speak to, no clean clothes and no toothbrush. In order to help time pass I did everything v-e-r-y s-l-o-w-l-y. I made tea slowly, drank it slowly, dressed slowly. I found a small free sample of face cream in my bag and applied it – slowly. I really wished I had a toothbrush.

To amuse myself I started to write a detailed description of the flat:

> *The bathroom has no sink, the plumbing is exposed and there is a bucket next to the toilet for the loo paper. Brown wallpaper with burn marks covers the walls and a folded-up curtain covers the floor. The focal point is a box of matches and a lighter.*

'Why matches and a lighter in the bathroom?' I asked myself.

By now, after several weeks in Pavlodar, in the northeast of Kazakhstan, nothing should have surprised me. The simple puzzle of a box of matches and a lighter in a bathroom should not have fazed me at all. At least it was something tangible on which to focus rather than on the quite desperate situation of being locked in this flat. I was becoming more and more claustrophobic, lonely, desperately lonely, depressed and beside myself with frustration. These were feelings with which I had become all too familiar and which would stay with me until I finally returned home.

Several friends and family members frequently asked why I did not return home before the year-end. My response was simply that I can be stubborn, to which many people would testify, but also that I took a certain pride in wanting to complete the year's contract I had agreed with the agency.

The answer to the other frequently asked question (Why did you go in the first place?) was not so easy.

'You're going where?' my boss exclaimed, making no attempt to disguise the incredulity in his voice.

'Kazakhstan,' I repeated quietly.

'And tell me again, what is it you're going to do?' Now there was some annoyance alongside the incredulity.

'I've been accepted as a volunteer to work in a drug treatment centre there,' I said.

The enormity of my decision was beginning to dawn on me. What on earth was I thinking, giving up my good job as therapist and manager in a well-respected addiction treatment centre, selling my car, storing all my worldly belongings in a garage and renting out my house; all at the ripe old age of fifty-seven? What exactly was driving me to give up a comfortable lifestyle and leave my four children, three grandchildren, mother, sister and friends? Was it a somewhat delayed midlife crisis? Possibly.

At this stage I had been divorced for more than ten years, had then been in a volatile yet beautiful relationship which had come to an extremely painful end, had survived breast cancer and felt my children were quietly getting on with their lives without my constant intervention.

'Nothing is forever' is a phrase which comes to mind. I could no longer take for granted my relationships, nor my health. If life was going to jump up and give me a kick up the backside then I needed to take notice and respond. I had always wanted to travel more, ever since my husband and I had spent two years in Sierra Leone, many years before. However, my husband, being a very responsible and sensible man, had decided we needed to settle in England and provide a safe and secure home for our children. So that is what we did. But these children were now in their late twenties and thirties and building their own version of how life should be. Maybe now was the right time for me to indulge my dream of travelling and exploring more of the world. Had I not had a big shove in that direction?

Little did I realise just how much of a challenge it would be.

IN THE BEGINNING

I had just bid a sad and tearful farewell to my beautiful daughters at Heathrow airport and so I was very happy to see Tom (another volunteer I had met at an induction course a month before) in the queue for checking-in.

'Who do you think the other volunteer is?' I whispered as I scanned the other travellers in the queue.

'I'm not sure. Perhaps the guy near the front with the rucksack?' ventured Tom.

'Possibly,' I said, 'but do you feel like going and asking him?'

'Hey,' whispered Tim, 'do you have a pen and some paper? We could write his name and show it around.'

After rummaging in my rucksack, I finally produced the said articles and we duly wrote his name. Tom, being above average height, held it aloft. Initially everyone looked away, embarrassed, but then a young man shyly sidled over to introduce himself and his friend to us. His friend was Mike and it was Mike who was the volunteer, but Mike clearly thought he was going to have nothing to do with us. However, he had little choice and we soon lost our initial shyness and were chatting away excitedly.

And so it was we set off with some trepidation and excitement on our journey into the unknown.

Two

INDUCTION

On our arrival at Almaty (the erstwhile capital of Kazakhstan) in the early hours of the morning and still dark, we were met by Nessar, who was one of the staff members in the volunteer office. She efficiently shepherded us into taxis and delivered us to the apartments which were to be our homes for the two weeks' stay in Almaty.

As is usual for me on arriving in any new city, I could not wait to set off and explore. I called for Tom and Mike to see whether they wanted to join me. Tom did not but Mike did, so we set off on foot without even thinking to write down where we were staying. Did we even know? I think not!

Our first impressions were that there were, surprisingly, lots of trees, and many shops and kiosks, but it was not always easy to tell what they were selling. The shop windows were not 'dressed' as ours are in the West. Again surprisingly, there were no smells, everywhere appeared to be very clean and thankfully, largely, we were ignored.

The streets were wide and set out in a grid pattern, so theoretically one could not get lost. But after two hours or so we realised we were totally and absolutely – lost! As time went on we realised we would have eat humble pie and call Nessar, since we were due to meet her at midday and we had no idea where we were. We made for a large supermarket so we could tell her where we could be found. We were embarrassed to make the call, but fortunately Nessar seemed to find it all quite amusing.

Thus our induction to Kazakhstan and to the volunteer programme began. Our time in Almaty turned out to be pretty hectic. Our group of four from the UK (myself – an addictions counsellor – plus a social worker, project manager and probation officer) were joined by two ladies from the Philippines (both social workers – though that term means different things in different countries, we have discovered). Our induction each morning consisted of learning about the volunteer programme office in Kazakhstan, meeting with a number of partner organisations with whom the organisation worked, visiting a few of the projects currently running and having meetings with our individual placement managers. We also had three hours of Russian language tuition each afternoon.

One visit to the British Council library was followed by lunch during which we had time for an interesting conversation with one of the volunteer officers, a lovely Kazakh lady. She told us she had married at the ripe old age of twenty-eight as she was fed up with being described as a spinster! That was twenty years ago and she was very happy. She told us that the older Kazakhs had been happier in the Soviet times, since they had been provided with free education, accommodation, medical services, jobs for all and help for the poor. The first years after Perestroika had been extremely difficult and it had taken a long time to build up the infrastructure. This was a vast understatement, I later learned.

One day we were all to meet our respective managers over lunch. It turned out to be a somewhat chaotic, noisy occasion, with six different conversations taking place, through interpreters mostly, both volunteers and managers desperately trying to make good impressions whilst at the same time weighing each other up. Lily, my manager was a very attractive, smartly dressed woman in her early forties who was accompanied by a young man who seemed to be some kind of lackey – he attended to her every need, including carrying her handbag. To say she had delusions of grandeur would not be too harsh. Having said that, my first impression was quite favourable. She seemed to be trying to ensure I would have everything I needed, although she herself had business in Almaty and would not be travelling to Pavlodar, where I was to go to work once the induction period was over, for another two or three weeks.

Afternoons, as I said, were for Russian lessons. Aida was a great teacher, both in stature and skill, though I fear we disappointed her with our language skills. On the middle Saturday she took all six of us to the very crowded market to help us learn to ask for things, find out how much they cost and barter. What a brave lady! She then took us to the park to finish that day's lesson. The park commemorates the blunting of the Nazi advance in that area in 1941, when Russian/Kazakh soldiers, realising they were outnumbered and insufficiently armed and therefore about to be overwhelmed by the German tanks, strategically exploded their tanks – and themselves. A huge memorial (they do like their huge statues) was erected in this park, and it is now tradition that wedding parties go there after the civil ceremony to pay their respects and have photos taken – so throughout our lesson there were numerous wedding parties wandering around, which was quite bizarre.

We also met some of the current volunteers who took us out; for example, on a trip up to the mountains. This involved riding in one of their mini buses, in which people seemed to constantly attempt to break the world record for the number of people riding at any one time. Lunch was taken, in yes! – a yurt: a tent, in effect, with a hole in the top for the smoke from the fire to escape. Carpets lined the walls and, in deference to visitors, low stools were provided whilst we ate. The traditional food was very meaty, probably horse meat: not at all appealing. Being vegetarian, I opted for a Greek style salad; of course it was nothing like a Greek salad but was edible and reasonably tasty.

We took the chair lift up a further two thousand, five hundred feet and I was shocked, though should not have been, to find just how much colder it was up there. I was freezing (the temperature had been about twenty-five degrees in Almaty when we had left, about midday), which was not really surprising when we saw there was snow up there! The two Filipino ladies had opted not to take the chair lift, and so we carefully carried a snowball back to the bottom to show them. They had not seen snow before and were quite bemused.

Anyway, it was lovely and a welcome change from the city. We walked back down the mountain and all of us suffered sore legs the next day. In fact the Filipino ladies could hardly walk, but they had some strange oil which they massaged themselves with and then they seemed to recover quickly.

We were also taken to a club where live bands played every night, which was great. I very much enjoyed having a good jig around to some familiar music, though sharing the dance floor with so many 'working girls' was an interesting experience. They viewed us with some mistrust, and I felt I wanted to reassure them that I was not going to take business away from them.

Almaty itself, whilst no longer the capital (though the foreign embassies are still based there), is a curious mixture of European and Soviet influences. The centre is very European, with extremely expensive shops, some of them with designer names, and lots of cafes and restaurants. Just off the centre are many apartment blocks and evidence of poverty. Sadly here, as in so many other places, one sees evidence of the 'haves' and 'have-nots'. Hence a visit to the ballet was definitely an experience for the 'haves'.

The theatre was glorious, the interior being made of marble with fantastic lighting provided by chandeliers, the decor was sumptuous. The audience was dressed to match. The women were extremely smartly dressed with flawless makeup. This was my first exposure to the gaping gap between the genders. The men, compared to their wives, were quite scruffy. It was also my first time experiencing the very civilised system of leaving one's coat, and later, when the snow lay thick on the ground, boots also, in a cloakroom. The ballet itself was *Swan Lake*, not my favourite but beautifully performed, and the costumes and scenery were fantastic.

We volunteers were then treated to a fabulous Chinese meal. I probably appreciated it the most because, as a vegetarian, I was already finding the food somewhat bland and boring.

As I took in the city and examined, as closely as I dared, the faces of people in the street, I saw that they appeared to be of very mixed races. Immigrants from Germany and other eastern European countries and many parts of Russia over the years have provided an interesting mix of features. The Kazakh girls are so stunning, they must surely rank as some of the most beautiful in the world. Walking down the street with Tom and Mike became embarrassing, and so I resorted to linking arms with them to keep them moving and to stop them ogling. Furthermore, I felt demoralised by the attention the girls paid to their dress and makeup; it left me feeling dowdy. They were incredibly vain, though, and never missed an opportunity to look at their reflections in mirrors and shop windows. Yet the same could certainly not be said of the Kazakh men. 'How can this possibly be, that the daughters turn out to be stunning and yet the same features in the sons have a totally different effect?' I asked myself many a time!

Otherwise, my impression of the Kazakhs so far was that they were quite distant, standoffish, and direct, but once you could engage in any more meaningful interaction, they were are warm and friendly. However, it was still early days and meaningful interactions were as yet few and far between, as very few spoke English and my Russian did not extend beyond the very basic, which was recited in a minute or two.

The day before we left Almaty we were taken to the huge outdoor market to buy our *dublonkas* (heavy fur coats) and boots to match. We took the bus, bursting at the seams as usual and very stuffy. All was fine until we hit a traffic jam caused by faulty traffic lights. With everyone jostling for road space, there was complete chaos. Our driver got the idea to cross the central reservation and head back the way we had come. This was obviously not a decision with which many of the passengers agreed, so he did another U-turn and proceeded down the wrong side of the dual carriageway – as did many others! We arrived in one piece eventually, and embarked on a very tiring process of buying *dublonkas*, boots, hats and gloves for all four of us.

On the last night in Almaty, I had a very disconcerting dream in which my children told me there were things they had not said to me and that actually they were quite glad I was leaving. I woke up crying. Naturally I found this very upsetting, but probably the dream was my unconscious working through the anxiety and apprehension I was having to deal with.

Our induction period came to an end and four of us, plus Nessar, boarded a train in Almaty at eight p.m. on the Sunday evening for a three-day trip to the northeast of the country. We woke to our first view of the steppe – a wild expanse of flat nothingness, except for the occasional building, goat herd and small hillock. We spent the next two days in a four-berth compartment, eating, consuming a little vodka, dozing, playing cards and chatting. When we stopped at a station (always at the scheduled time) we would alight, sometimes buy food and drink from the sellers, stretch our legs and then re-embark. Hot drinks could be made by taking hot water from the samovar attended to by the compartment attendant. Washing the cups was a risky affair, as the only available water was in the toilets. The state of cleanliness of these toilets depended on the vigilance and diligence of the attendants, and consequently was variable. It was not the most comfortable journey I have ever taken but it was not the worst either.

Mike disembarked at Astana and I was sad to see him go. I had enjoyed his company.

Thirty-six hours later at six a.m., and a thousand miles further north and therefore much, much colder, we arrived in a dull, grey, cold and very uninviting Pavlodar.

Main pedestrianised street Almaty

View of mountains in Almaty

In the Alatau mountains

Three

LIFE BEGINS IN PAVLODAR

We were met by representatives of our organisations, plus one or two interpreters, but it was all quite confusing and I had no idea who was who. I was brought to an apartment with my 'director', Vadim (quite what he was directing was not altogether clear yet), and Anya, who apparently was my interpreter and who had only just graduated in English and German.

We were greeted by my landlady and neighbour, who had clearly been told to feed me, so we were given bread and cheese and strawberry jam and tea. We then had a three-way discussion as to what I was to have for my dinner, and decided on mashed potato and a sort of ratatouille (my not eating meat was met with a very quizzical look), which was duly served about an hour later. I attempted to thank the landlady profusely and reassure her that she did not need to cook for me – mainly as I was anxious about having to pay her, which on less than two hundred dollars a month would be stretching it somewhat.

I was then taken to the drug rehabilitation centre, a seven-storey building. I was completely taken aback to find it extremely well equipped and laid out with everything from medical rooms, including scanning equipment; laboratories where they read their own drug tests amongst other medical tests; departments for psychology, radiography, physiotherapy, research and publishing; and leisure facilities including a banya, a gym, table-tennis tables on most floors, a relaxation room and a sensory room. This latter had a number of different laser-type lamps and other interesting lighting, with music and special chairs, plus numerous other extras which I have probably forgotten. The idea, I think, was to stimulate feelings and relaxation. I suspect it was more likely to induce hallucinations!

I did see a few patients, but nowhere near the one hundred I was told were currently resident. Their rooms were, on average, four bedded, but quite cramped, with only a small bedside table for each and no screens of any description. I saw one or two patients waiting to be admitted and another couple in the medical department; others were watching an educational video and a few more were in group therapy. Overall, my impression was of a well-equipped clinic, very clinical but not at all homely.

Patients stayed in the first stage (which I understood to be the detoxification wing) for about three weeks, then moved up a floor for their second stage, which lasted two months. Third stage was housed in another property some thirty kilometres away. There was some confusion still as to where I would be based. It seemed my manager was the manager of the third stage (and, incidentally, the wife of the overall director). She said I would be based in Pavlodar and spend some time in the third stage, but today the deputy director seemed to be implying something else.

I found that I was expected to do a presentation tomorrow morning for some fifteen doctors. This had to be a non-starter –even if I could prepare a presentation, I doubted poor Anya would be able to interpret such a thing yet. Fortunately at lunchtime we met up with Nessar, the volunteer staff member who had accompanied us on the train, and she put them straight in no uncertain terms – well, I think that was what she was doing! Nessar suggested we all wait for my 'boss' to return from her trip to Almaty on 7 October, which suited me fine as I really needed to find my way around the city – get used to the buses and trams, and find the shops and market!

A few hours later saw me feasting on bread and peanut butter and honey for dinner (maybe I should have let my landlady cook for me?) after a frustrating hour trying to call the UK – without success again. On the plus side, my laptop was working, though I could not access the internet as yet. But as I listened to Paul McCartney, I decided the speakers were worth every kilogram they weighed and I was still glad I had brought them rather than more shoes, as the shoes could be replaced at a fraction of the cost. Also, on the plus side my apartment was better than expected.

I was on the fourth floor of a very typical Soviet-type apartment block. The usual layout was for three blocks to surround a children's playground – varying greatly in quality and in no way comparing with British parks! The entrances to the flats were very unprepossessing, the stairwells somewhat bleak, often smelling of urine and stale cooking amongst other things, and the steel doors that most apartments seemed to have were not reassuring.

The interiors were decorated in rather interesting, embossed wallpaper, and the floors were covered in linoleum with a scattering of rugs. The furniture was reminiscent of my grandparents' houses in England in the 1950s and the cooker was even more antiquated, but all was functional – just!

The telephone system left a lot to be desired – local calls were free but national and international calls were not at all consistent. We had no hot water until the heating was turned on by the central government office on 1 October. So washing myself and my clothes was an interesting experience that entailed heating water on the one working cooker ring and sluicing down in the bath, banya style. Apparently in the villages there are communal, though gender-separated, banyas where water is heated perhaps once a week and all strip off and lather down, helping each other and then tipping bowls of water over themselves! I was taken to a public banya in Almaty which also had saunas and steam rooms and a small but cold swimming pool. I treated myself to a massage – an exfoliating one which was more invigorating than relaxing. The *piece de resistance* was beating each other with myrtle leaves – very exhilarating!

Four

LOCKED OUT – AND IN

The temperature was slowly dropping – it was now down to zero, but quite bright and sunny. I had heating in the bedroom, but the powers-that-be had obviously decided heating was not necessary in the sitting room and kitchen at the moment. The water heater was on and the water was hot – very hot – which meant that, due to the low pressure on the cold tap, taking a shower was, shall we say interesting: it entailed leaping in and out of the spray, as the temperature fluctuated frequently. Baths were probably safer, but I had to be organised well in advance to achieve a satisfactory temperature.

I had several sleepless nights feeling upset, as I had not been able to phone home and desperately wanted to speak to my children. The phone card I had bought did not seem to work, and whilst I had tried to explain to my problem Anya, she either did not understand or, due to her tender years, had no clue as to how to help.

After a shopping trip to get some household objects, Anya and I returned, feeling very weary, only to find the lock had jammed and we could not get in. My landlady appeared from next door, which was also her apartment, and managed eventually to free the lock. We got in only to find she had removed the coffee table, hall table, TV, phone and bits and pieces from the kitchen. I was not happy. She obviously had a key, but I had not expected her to walk in and out whenever she wanted, let alone remove furniture without telling or asking me. The language barrier did not help, but I got the feeling she probably would not bother to explain even if I spoke Russian. I guess she just saw it as her right to treat my apartment as her own, paying no attention to my privacy or security.

It was arranged for me to visit the third stage centre – Acar. We travelled in a minibus and I got to see a bit more of the city. Parts of it struck me as quite attractive – like the riverbank, which has a huge promenade. The roads were wide, if somewhat pitted, and so the van lurched from side to side as we avoided the potholes.

The landscape beyond the city was boring. Acar, however, was interesting, set in the middle of nowhere (so little chance of the patients 'escaping'!) alongside the river. It was run more or less as a therapeutic community.

Anya and I were taken on what they insisted on calling an 'excursion', a tour of the building and grounds. The rooms were four-bedded and sparse, but with slightly more space than those at the main centre. In a separate building was a billiard room, sewing room, computer room, studio with mini gym and a banya, of course. In addition there were a few animals – cows, a bull, sheep, chickens – for some of the residents to take care of. A couple of cottages were used for storage whilst the third seemed to be used as an occasional overnight stop for staff or visitors. Someone casually remarked it was to be my room. This was not going to happen. There was no way I wanted to be based so far from the town, with no private bathroom and, in all probability, no privacy and time for myself. No doubt all would be revealed when my boss arrived.

We were then shown 'the video', which showed how the centre was rebuilt to its present condition. Next came a meeting with the other members of staff.

'Why are you coming here to our centre?' one psychologist asked. (I later realised these psychologists do not have the training that psychologists in the West have. I considered them to be less than well qualified counsellors, but of course I did not voice my thoughts.)

'What is your role here?' another one asked.

Thinking frantically on my feet, I replied, 'So we can exchange ideas as to the best way of treating addicts and alcoholics.' And then, to change the focus, I said, 'Can you tell me a little about the programme here?'

I was then given a detailed account of their version of a therapeutic community. It was similar to how we understand therapeutic communities in the West, whereby the residents are encouraged to manage the running of the 'home' on their own with the support of the staff, who have ultimate responsibility. However, as I was to discover in time, the reality at Acar was quite different.

We were asked to stay for dinner, and given that the bus was not due back into Pavlodar for half an hour or so, this seemed like a good idea. The residents were intrigued by us – well, I suspect by Anya really, as she is very beautiful!

The next day I went for a lovely walk down by the river with Anya, after which we ambled back to my flat. Tom called and invited me to go with him and one of his colleagues to see the mosque. It is huge and from the outside looks a bit like Darth Vader's helmet. It is, in fact, the largest in Kazakhstan and one of the largest in the world.

On entering, we ladies had to don cloaks and hoods before being taken on a tour. From the first floor we looked down on the praying area, which of course is bare except for carpet and a fabulous chandelier. The area can take fifteen hundred men – the women of course have a separate room. It was pretty impressive and I found the simplicity spiritually uplifting.

I went back with Tom to his flat, which was smaller and even more basic than mine. This did not seem to bother him much, so why should it bother me? He discovered he did not even have a corkscrew and so we were creative in removing the cork from the wine bottle. He was going to cook spaghetti Bolognese, but as he only had the one ring this took an awfully long time and we were quite drunk by the time food was ready. This, of course, in no way detracted from our enjoyment of the food.

A few days later, we made another cultural visit, this time to the orthodox church. Of course, places of worship are somewhat new buildings, having only been erected three years ago – since Glasnost. The Orthodox Church is a more beautiful building on the outside than the mosque, but very ornate inside and, for me, not as moving. We also took in the Cultural Centre, and this being Celebration Day (seven hundred and fifty years since the founding of Pavlodar), there were displays of children dancing and singing.

On returning to my flat, I found the lock jammed again. I called Anya, who called Vadim who decided I should go and wait at his flat.

So off Anya and I went. Vadim kindly cooked a tasty meal of rice, stir-fry, tomato salad and various mixed vegetables from a jar. I was surprised that neither Vadim nor Anya were eating with me, and asked why that was.

'Ah,' said Vadim, 'I go now to party. I return tomorrow to fix the lock. Here is bedroom, bathroom. Please be comfortable. I lock door now and see you tomorrow.'

And with that, off they both went.

By now it should not be too difficult to understand the loneliness and frustration I described earlier – strange flat, God knows where, with nothing to do, no-one to speak to, no clean clothes and so on.

Come ten thirty a.m. I had demolished what was left of some delicious homemade raspberry jam with the bread left from last night. I found some toothpicks and did my best with those!

By midday, just as I was running out of ideas to amuse myself, there was a knock at the door. Despite Vadim having locked the door I could actually open it from inside, although as I had no idea where I was it was of little comfort. I tentatively opened the door. It was a neighbour. Through brilliant sign language and a bit of Russian, I understood that a piece of her washing had blown off her balcony onto Vadim's windowsill and she wanted to retrieve it. Being short, she was unable to reach it, so I leant out with her holding my legs and managed to reach her panties. Well, it passed a few entertaining minutes.

Finally, at twelve thirty, Vadim, Anya and Irlan (another 'volunteer') arrived. We went to my flat. They had not been able to open the door so had called in the professionals, who arrived with ropes. One guy went up to the top of the building and onto the roof from which he belayed down to my balcony, watched by many a bemused neighbour. He smashed the balcony door open and entered the flat. Hooray!

An hour later they returned with a new lock and fitted it. Now, how to stay free of any more jammed locks? And why did it keep jamming anyway? One of life's mysteries, I feared, but I was concerned it should not happen again. Each time I went out I did not want to wonder not only whether my landlady would go in again but also whether I would be able to get in again.

It did happen again, and this time Vadim was able to free the lock by jiggling. He then mentioned that I had to turn the lock twice when locking, not just the once. Why had no one told me that before? At least that was one puzzle solved, and hopefully I would have no more problems. One can always choose positivity.

That evening I hit another low because a) I had still been unable to call the children; and b) the fact the cooker – well, the single ring that was working – had decided now not to work. So it was crackers and peanut butter for dinner again.

The next day, I decided to go to the market to buy some things for the flat, only to remember, as I got off the tram, that it was Monday and there was no market. So I returned and found some of the things I wanted in a little local shop. I then had to wait in for someone to come and fix my cooker. I was totally bored, and could not go out (and had nowhere to go anyway). Eventually the long-suffering Vadim appeared with an engineer, who flicked the trip switch and – hey presto! – now the whole cooker worked. So I set to preparing a tasty meal, only to find the trip switch kept going if I used more than one ring. After several trips, I managed to get some hot food.

Later that evening, I was paid a visit by my landlady and her daughter. I had not taken to these ladies; I did not trust them as they obviously came into the flat when I was not there and this did not make me feel comfortable.

'You have spare key?' Andrea, the landlady's daughter, demanded.

'Sorry, I do not understand,' I said.

'Keys for apartment – you have two?' Andrea insisted.

'Yes, I have two,' I replied, not sure where this was going.

'You give me one,' she demanded.

No way, I thought, and asked her, 'Why do you want it?'

'In case of problem,' she replied.

This did not make sense as I knew they already had a key and I was certainly not going to give them another one.

'No, no. I want my friend to have the other key,' I said.

'No, you give me key now,' Andrea repeated.

'No, no understand,' I told her, meaning I understood perfectly but no way would I give in to her.

Eventually they got the message and left, leaving me somewhat bemused and more than a little angry. I already shared a phone line with the daughter in the adjoining flat, which was problematic as she always answered when it rang and did not necessarily wait for me to pick up if it was for me. So I stopped answering altogether, only to find the next day that Tom had been trying to call me all evening.

View of river and esplanade Pavlodar

Pavlodar's Mosque

Orthodox church, Pavlodar

Breaking into my flat

Five

A Trip to the Hospital

My social life was meagre; to be honest, non-existent. This did not help the feelings of loneliness and isolation. The only people I ever talked to were Anya and, occasionally, Vadim when I had a problem, and Tom of course.

I wanted to thank Anya and Vadim for helping me out. I had now worked out that Vadim was a fairly newly recovering addict who was doing some voluntary work for the centre – not a director at all! By the way, the term 'volunteer' was causing some confusion. Patients who had completed their treatment and who wanted to stay around were given some work, usually outreach-type projects, talking to other addicts and telling them how wonderful treatment was. I was also a volunteer, but in all modesty had several qualifications and many years' experience, which I had hoped to share. So the confusion was held not only by myself but by everyone else, and no doubt contributed to the lack of clarity as to my role.

Anyway I invited Vadim and Anya for lunch and then we were all going ice-skating. I cooked up some of my soya stuff, which I thought was quite tasty which they made a very valiant attempt to eat. Vadim had brought a box of delicious little coconut and cream cakes, so we had those to fill up on if they had not enjoyed the soya.

I had taken to heart the message on a coaster given to me as a present when I left England and decided ice-skating would help me shake off the illusion of age! So we took the tram, and chose our skates and, after I waved Anya and Vadim off, I set off, clinging to the barrier. I declined their kind offers of help and as my courage increased I started to do the circuits unaided.

All was well until I fell – on my sacrum and coccyx, and I guess my wrist took the brunt of it. The pain was excruciating, especially in my *derriere*, so I limped, with gritted teeth and bitten lips, off the ice. After resting for a little while I decided, a bit like horse riding, to get back on the ice. Big mistake! After the second identical fall, Anya expertly glided over to check on me. I did try to smile but I think it probably came out like a grimace, and I showed her my now rapidly swelling wrist and hand. She called the first aid people, whose response was to fit a sling and order a car on the house to take me home. What an ignominious experience!

After a painful night, my wrist showed no improvement; in fact, it was even more swollen and completely useless, and the pain in my *derriere* caused me to limp somewhat. That afternoon, on meeting my boss in the corridor (we rarely had scheduled meetings), she decided that a visit to the hospital was necessary. I was not altogether happy with this, having grave misgivings about what the hospital might have to offer.

The building was again a curious mixture of 1950s-type architecture and decor, but the equipment looked quite modern. Having been sent by my boss, I was given immediate attention, which was a relief and yet embarrassing at the same time. It was a while since I had been in an X-ray department, but the machinery looked pretty modern to me and the techniques used were as I remembered from all those years ago in my former life as a radiographer.

It seemed I had chipped the end of my ulna, though when I looked at the X-rays I thought it looked more like the ends of both radius and ulna had compacted. So off I went to have a half-plaster put on, which did not feel very firm and so I did not feel very reassured.

All this might seem bad enough, but then I should explain that the damaged wrist was my left one and guess which is my dominant hand? So now I was seriously struggling with washing and showering, dressing, preparing food, cooking, washing up and hand-washing my clothes! Whilst everything seemed hard before, now it was even harder, and I had to admit I was reduced to tears on many an occasion. The frustration I had felt before was nothing compared to the current feeling. There is no knack to cutting up vegetables with one hand. It is well-nigh impossible. There is no knack to wringing out wet clothes one handed. It is impossible. Showering and dressing were possible, but took so long I now had to get up much earlier to get ready for work. Self-pity called at my door, big time.

Work-wise I had now observed a 'training', which is what they called group/workshop – a strange combination of the two. This was the first session for the 'psychologist' with this particular group and this group was the most dedicated, electing to take a cold shower each morning, go for an early morning run and give up smoking, and setting other strict rules. All quite bizarre! I noticed that the concept 'a day at a time' did not appear on their agenda, nor did focusing on 'here and now' feelings, both of which are the main focus in the UK and very good mantras for those in early recovery.

So my first session at the centre was planned and, how thoughtful, I was given the graveyard slot after lunch (when everyone is sleepy and not inclined to do anything, let alone group therapy). It turned out to be the most difficult group therapy I have ever attempted. I had already realised that it was going to be well-nigh impossible to execute group therapy as such, due to the totally different approach of not helping the patients access their feelings. Added to that was the time lapse whilst Anya interpreted for both myself and the patients. It was not at all productive, in my view, and both Anya and I were exhausted. I had to tune in so much more to body language, intonation and general presentation than I would normally, in order to gain a sense of any underlying emotion. By the end I had a headache.

After several more of these sessions with two different groups, I attempted to introduce them to family systems (my specialist area and one which I had hoped to be focusing on) and help them explore and understand their own family dynamics. However, I found holding the attention of recently detoxed patients in the graveyard slot whilst working through an interpreter who was still struggling with some of the terminology something of a challenge, to put it mildly. At least one patient, though, said it was good to be talking about families, as this did not usually happen!

A challenge it might have been, but it was not exactly what I expected to be doing – working directly with the patients. A volunteer's role, as I had understood it, was to share ideas and techniques with those working in a similar situation and assist in adopting any new ideas which they may wish to take on board. It was becoming quite clear that this had not been communicated to the staff, and I did not know whether this was a miscommunication between my boss and the rest of the staff or my superiors and my boss. In my brief conversations with the staff they appeared to be expecting me to produce a magic wand and show them the easy technique for 'curing addiction'!

When I looked at their treatment programme and all the different aspects to it, I got the strong feeling they had included everything they had ever read or seen in the hope that something would stick. Furthermore, they also seemed quite happy with the results. Now these results were somewhat elusive. I asked repeatedly for statistics on the number of patients admitted, how long they stayed in treatment and what percentage stayed in remission for two years or more. Despite the research department being very professional, these figures were not available. When some figures were finally produced, they were, unsurprisingly, not reassuring, though all the staff I spoke to seem very pleased and proud of their achievements. In some ways, so they should have been. They were trying to deal with a monumental problem. There was no aftercare of any description and so the patients returned to their family homes, to exactly the same situation in which they had been using. Not a good way to start recovery.

The usual route to addiction in Kazakhstan is to be introduced to heroin at a very young age – forget the slower Western route through alcohol, cannabis, speed, hallucinogens, uppers and downers through to heroin, cocaine, crack and so on. Heroin from Afghanistan is plentiful and cheap, hence the very young age of addicts in treatment, mostly thrust there by (understandably very worried) well-off parents. Kazakhstan is a huge country, the ninth largest in the world and the largest landlocked country. The patients at the centre were brought there from their homes, often hundreds of miles away, and once they returned there was no support for them and no help for the families. One can easily imagine parents attempting to exert very strong control over their youngsters when they returned home and the children having little option to escape this control but to seek out the one thing the parents could not control: their drugs.

One day, after several weeks of trying, I finally managed to arrange a meeting with some of the psychologists to share ideas and philosophies. Two turned up, another came late and one left after a few minutes. So how was I to do what I thought I was required to do – to help identify what changes they may want to make and then help them make them? I was increasingly getting the feeling I was staring at the north face of the Eiger with a group who thought they were already beyond base camp and did not realise just how far they were from the summit and that those they were trying to take with them did not even want to go.

Of course, had I been able to speak their language it might have been somewhat easier. I could never have learned Russian well enough to speak fluently with the staff or patients but it would certainly have helped. I wanted to build on the lessons we had with the wonderful Aida in Almaty. However, this was Pavlodar and not Almaty, and there was not much call for Russian teachers. I made many enquiries, all to no avail. Then I found a teacher called Umut, who was a somewhat formidable lady. I do not think she had taught an Englishwoman before, and her lessons, whilst not a complete waste of time, focused too much on the grammar and not enough on speaking. I have to confess, though, I was a little in awe of her, so the lessons were not a comfortable experience. Learning a language late in life is a big challenge and is exhausting.

I returned home after one such lesson to find the lock had jammed again. This was the final straw. I was going to find another flat. Control was taken out of my hands, though I suspect my manager believed she was helping. Vadim took me to inspect the flat he and Lily had chosen, and I was not sure how much say I actually had. I did not have a clue where it was in relation to anywhere else, and it was much smaller and full of smoke, but it did have its own telephone – oh joy! – and good water pressure. So I was to sign the contract and move in three days.

My good luck knew no bounds: when I returned home, my sister called, and for once my neighbour did not pick up the phone first. It was so good to talk to her. I missed my family so much, especially their support, which I greatly needed. Mr Self Pity reigned supreme at the moment, and trying to type letters home with one hand was tedious in the extreme.

Typical street in Pavlodar

River Irtysh, Pavlodar, in winter

Digging out

Six

ANOTHER SHOCK

The temperature was down to minus ten, but as it was bright and sunny it was quite acceptable. The flats and offices and even the individual seats on the trams were well heated, so as long as I didn't stay outside for too long, it was just possible not to freeze – so far!

Having mentioned the trams, I thought I would just say something about the transport. In Pavlodar there are buses, trams and *bashookas* (minibuses) – none of which run to any timetable but they are fairly regular. The *bashookas* make for an interesting ride as there seems to be no restriction as to how many people they should carry, which can be a bit scary. For example, one evening I was travelling home from the library and more and more people crammed in, so much so I could not see a thing outside. I could not tell where we were and began to panic slightly, as if I went past my stop, I did not think I would ever find my way back! I counted the stops and made what turned out to be an accurate guess, and was very thankful to find myself home. You really don't want to be wandering around outside for any longer than is absolutely necessary!

The most one pays on any of these *bashookas* is 20 tenge, which is less than ten pence, for any journey, no matter how long. One pays the money to the driver, who manages to count it and send change back via whoever is between you and him, whilst negotiating the road and the other dreadful drivers (I often wondered whether any of them had passed a driving test – I later learned that driving licences, like many other things such as degrees, can be bought).

Some of the buses are 1950s in style and certainly they look and sound as if they have not been updated – at all. They are unbelievably shaky, noisy, smelly and drafty and, well, just ancient. As you climb on board, you notice the lady perched on the dashboard next to the driver. She is there to take your money as you get off and has change all ready in a pile on the sort-of dashboard – very efficient!

Then there are the trams, which obviously have limited routes but are very efficient and, as mentioned before, the seats are individually heated. Now that is a real treat!

Another cheap commodity is medicine. When I had run out of paracetamol (I seemed to be getting rather a lot of headaches; cannot understand why!), I asked Anya to recommend some headache tablets. She did, and said they were about ten tenge. When I asked for twenty (thinking it was ten tenge a tablet), she laughed – it was for a packet of ten! They later proved to be perfectly effective.

My arm was still in plaster and one of the highlights was another visit to the hospital. Well, I needed lots of distractions! My plaster had been feeling extraordinarily loose and I could not believe it was doing anything like holding the broken bits together. So I showed it to what I thought was the nurse – of course, it might well have been a cleaner, for all I knew – who removed the grubby top layer of bandage and put a new bandage over the plaster. A very effective cure, I am sure.

Anyway, thinking I might capitalise on this visit, I asked the nurse and the doctor who was also there why my face was all swollen on one side. I had woken up that morning feeling something was wrong. Imagine my horror and shock when, looking in the mirror, I saw that one side of my face was swollen to the size of a football. I had no pain or discomfort other than that which the stretching was causing, and whilst I am not particularly vain, it was nevertheless very distressing. The doctor washed his hands before plunging them into my mouth, and then announced it was probably a dental problem. I had no chance to disagree with him!

He immediately went into ER mode, quite bizarrely, leaving me to believe it was a dire emergency. He told me to follow him, and we went flying down the corridor, up the stairs, along another corridor and into the X-ray department (yes, again) whereupon an X-ray was taken of my mouth this time. Off we flew again, along another corridor, up more stairs and this time into a dentist's room. The doctor thrust the X-ray into the dentist's hand and they had an animated discussion, presumably over the state of my mouth.

The dentist turned and told me to sit, at which point I was on the verge of panic as I thought he was about to extract a tooth there and then, and I had already spied some very nasty instruments on a tray. They assured me the dentist just wanted to look.

Sharp intakes of breath followed, and then, 'Vere did you get ze crown done?' This was followed by grave head shaking. 'No problem – ve take out ze tooth.'

'But not now, thank you very much,' I said, and I whipped the X-ray off them, said thank you again, *'desvedanya'*, (goodbye) and then left.

The next day I found another dentist (by now the swelling had almost gone). She looked at the X-ray and said, 'Yes? Vot is it you vant?'

'Well,' Anya explained for me, 'we were told she needed an extraction.'

'Why?' said the dentist. 'There is no problem here.'

I asked Anya to ask her why she thought my face had been swollen. The dentist said something to the effect, 'The swelling was probably just inflammation due to the cold. Don't worry!'

So I didn't, and that consultation cost me a whole pound!

After a session with Anya translating some handouts, we went to the centre and lunched on some pretty tasteless borsch. There were only four patients in the group today. It was so hard to keep any momentum going with patients who were sometimes there and sometimes not. Who knew where the other patients were or where they went. I certainly did not, and no explanation was ever given. I had to simply accept the situation and work with whoever turned up. Addicts are unpredictable, but this centre was run very much along prison lines and so they most certainly had not gone AWOL. The most likely answer was that they had been sent elsewhere, but where? Another puzzle to add to the many others.

Seven

Lily from Vogue

The day I was supposed to be moving came and went without anything happening. So I unpacked the things I had packed a few days earlier and spent a lonely and boring day. I called Tom and we met up for a walk and a drink. It did not do much to lift my low mood, and I went home for a bath and bed feeling very sorry for myself.

The next day, because it seemed the move to the other flat was not going to happen soon and I was feeling very ambivalent about it anyway, I called Anya and asked her to tell Vadim I was not happy with the new flat and wanted to stay in my present one as long as the phone was sorted out.

My landlady's daughter came round and showed me the switch under the phone for making international calls. Why, pray, had I had to wait so long for this information? And why on earth was there a switch under the phone with no indication as to what it was for?

Not being able to speak to my family had been one of the major upsets for me, and it was annoying that it had been unnecessary. I did not think this had been a communication problem; I could not but help think the landlady and her daughter were just downright thoughtless and rude.

As for work- I had a somewhat disastrous session with one group. I had decided to try a role play of a patient returning home and the likely interactions between themselves and other family members and friends. I had used a role play like this often in our centre in the UK and found it very useful for exploring possible problem situations. However, I found all too soon that role play is obviously not for the Kazakhs! They sabotaged it, making silly comments and laughing and interrupting each other. It might be that they were just not used to play-acting or using their imagination. Or perhaps it was a bit too close for comfort. On reflection, this is most likely, but disappointing nevertheless.

Socially, life was pretty dire. One evening I had planned to go out with Tom and some of his friends. Tom had been very fortunate in his placement with a small, friendly NGO with helpful staff, and his role as fundraiser was very clear. I waited for Tom for an hour. I tried to call but he did not answer. So I sat in feeling very silly, all dressed up with nowhere to go and, having drunk coffee, not at all sleepy.

I never did find out what had happened. Events occurred with such rapidity that by the time I saw Tom again I had forgotten all about it. However, as it happens, I was very glad they had not turned up in the end, as my daughter called me.

This was followed by an unusually busy weekend as Mike, the volunteer in Astana, came to visit. He came officially to see our wonderful treatment centre. His organisation referred addicts to the centre, so of course it made good sense to check it out. However, it made even more sense to come and see Tom and myself, catch up on our news and generally have a good moan to one another. He also needed help to celebrate his birthday – which we did our best to do in style, eating out, showing him the wonderful sites of Pavlodar and trying out a couple of the clubs. We also met up with a couple of American volunteers, so we had a little gang of us in the end. I felt quite sad when Mike left on Sunday evening for the overnight train back to Astana. It had been great to have his company and my flat felt very empty again once he'd gone and I was back to being alone… again.

At work, I decided it was high time to have a serious talk with my boss, Lily, as I was now feeling completely deskilled and useless and a misfit. However, meeting with her was not easy as I was not inclined to hang around the centre for hours, which was the usual procedure when you wanted to meet someone. I should explain that I had no office and no telephone, so I could not make any arrangements for a meeting. Instead, Anya and I would go to person's office and wait for them to find time to talk to me if they were there, or wait until they appeared from wherever they had been.

For example, on one occasion we waited to meet with the director of the research department. He was actually very friendly and welcoming and he had plenty to say, though not on the topics I wanted to discuss.

Stir Crazy in Kazakhstan

He insisted on offering us a little treat – a drink of fermented horse milk. I confess I only managed a few sips! It was quite disgusting; I am not a fan of cow's milk in the first place, let alone milk from any other animal. I really wanted to talk to him about outcomes and relapse rates and the like, but he was very evasive and I got nowhere.

Because I did not want to wait for her, I asked Anya to ring Lily (from another office) and ask for an appointment. I knew that was not normal here, but I thought it may be a tiny piece of time management I could introduce. I had no response for two days, and then nine thirty in the morning I was told she would see me at ten – it would take me a good half hour to get there and I was not ready. So I rushed around, washed, dressed, caught the bus and got there for five past ten, only to be told Lily was not there yet. I wanted to scream or run out of the building and never return, or both.

Anya and I had to wait in the reception area – as usual, once more increasing the feeling that I did not really have a position at the centre. Lily eventually swept in at about ten thirty with her little entourage (including, of course, the handbag carrier and general lackey and, one wonders, what else), as ever looking like someone out of *Vogue*: short black skirt with a frilly hem, a white sweater, white knee-length leather boots decorated with sparkly bits, a very expensive-looking black wool coat with fur trimmings and recently coiffured hair.

Actually I am being a tad unfair here, as many men carry their ladies' bags for them, so this is not unusual. What is a little unusual is that this man was not her husband; he was a former patient, and a fairly recent one at that!

Anyway, this imposing entrance and appearance was not for my benefit, of that I was sure. It was for a party of hard-nosed policemen who thought addicts were the scum of the earth and should be locked up forever. They were to visit Acar, the third-stage facility, for an 'excursion', as they called it, later that day, and to be shown the effectiveness of 'her' treatment.

Lily's glance finally fell on Anya and myself and she beckoned us to follow – so, like sheep, we joined the entourage, but finally we got to talk to her. Correction: she talked to me.

She told me she wanted me to work at Acar, now that I had spent time at the centre and found out about their methods. This was all well and good, but why had she chosen to withhold this information from me? In the face of her charming smile and the steely look in her eye, I had no choice but to concur. At least, I thought, I might be able to find something useful to do there. I certainly had not felt that so far.

So, I was to start tomorrow at Acar. The slight drawback was that the staff transport left at eight fifteen in the morning and did not leave Acar until six p.m., and the home trip could take well over an hour depending on who was dropped off first. So this was going to be a bit of shock to my system as the earliest I had been to work for so far was ten a.m.! Also, it completely messed up my Russian lessons. Still, nothing is ever perfect, and certainly not in Kazakhstan.

However, I had hardly started when I had to take a trip.

Eight

Sharing Skills

There was no sign of real snow. There remained evidence of the fall we'd had a couple of weeks ago, but in many places it had disappeared. It was quite cold, not unbearably so, but it did mean I had to walk like a very old lady to ensure I did not slip on the patches of ice which remained. I had become very cautious about walking on ice; I cannot imagine why!

Talking of which, I went to the hospital to have the plaster removed – the bones seem to have healed quite well but, disappointingly, my hand and wrist were still quite swollen and movement was restricted and a bit painful. So I was sent to see the physiotherapist at the centre, who put a couple of electrodes on my arm and passed some kind of current (as in electric, not dried fruit!) to take the swelling down, and I was told to soak my arm in salty water for twenty minutes – of course I did.

Anyway, it was so nice to be able to use my favourite hand again: to, joy of joys, be able to wash myself, my clothes and fruit, and cook, eat and so on without any restrictions.

Removal of the plaster happened at a good time as I then had to attend a skills share in a town called Semipalatinsk. This entailed a six-hour bus journey to the east of Pavlodar region. It was a get-together for all the volunteers in Kazakhstan, partly to socialise but also to do some work: namely to prepare the exit strategy as the voluntary organisation was due to pull out of Kazakhstan in March in two years' time. This seemed a bit premature to those of us who had only just arrived, but there you go.

The bus journey was uneventful, except that the untreated icy roads gave me some cause for concern. I coped by chatting or dozing – well, closing my eyes! We stopped once for about twenty minutes at a wayside cafe, practically the only building we saw for miles. The steppe was never-ending and unbelievably boring, but considerably prettier covered in snow. The stars were simply amazing. I had never seen so many, but then I had never been to a place so completely devoid of artificial light.

We stayed in what was laughingly described as a hotel. It was one of the old sanatoriums where the workers had been entitled to go for a week's 'holiday' in Soviet times. If it was as cold for them as it was for us, it was not much of a holiday. This was the first time I had felt cold since we arrived – the bedrooms felt like an icebox and the room we worked in was not much better. It was so cold that Tom and I decided we would have to share a bed in the hope we would not die of hypothermia in the night. We did not die, but it was not the most comfortable night, given that he is six foot two and the bed was less than three feet wide.

The food, in a word, was gross! I cannot describe adequately the unappetising, bland, badly cooked meals we were served. Being a vegetarian in a country devoted to eating meat, especially horse meat, was never going to be easy, but all that was offered to the three vegetarians was to pick out most of the meat from the soup or whatever the other dish was. Breakfast was mildly edible, so although I do not normally 'do' food so early in the day, I had to in order to exist!

On the first day we all had to do a very brief presentation to share how things were going for us. I decided to adapt John Lennon's 'Nobody told me there'd be days like these' for the occasion. I really warmed to the task once I started and was able to name most of my frustrations since arriving and, what's more, managed a pathetic attempt at singing. The song clearly struck a chord with several other volunteers, one of whom apologised afterwards for not joining in the chorus because she was too upset. It also prompted a response from the organisation's director, who approached me afterwards and said he had no idea things were so bad and asked what he could do to help. We set up a meeting later to discuss what could be done. I was grateful for the support but doubtful of any positive result.

We finished about three thirty on the last day, which just gave those of us from Pavlodar time to visit Dostoevsky's museum. This was interesting and well laid out, but disappointingly, there was no information in English. One of the volunteers who spoke good Russian was able to translate, but even so I grasped little of the detail. It made sufficient impact, however, for me to seek out his books again. Other than that, we saw little of Semey itself.

By the way, if the name Semipalatinsk sounds vaguely familiar, it may be because of the nuclear testing that went on there from 1949 to 1989. Four hundred and seventy nuclear bombs were exploded in an area just southwest of Semipalatinsk, obviously causing enormous health and environmental problems. Apparently, and unsurprisingly, the number of birth defects and cancers is extremely high in the area. No-one seems to know what the levels of radiation are like now, but one hopes they have resumed to safe levels, although I understand the incidence of birth defects remains worryingly high. Consequently fish was off limits as far as we were concerned.

The journey back was just as scary. I tried to sleep but could not relax. Tom was not in a talkative mood and the other volunteer based in Pavlodar) was not sitting near me, so I was left to my own, not so good, thoughts. We stopped for a twenty-minute break, and I wished I could photograph the women in their *dublonkas* and the men in their furry hats. The stars as before transported me somewhere else; they were amazing – so many and so beautiful.

Back at work I was summoned to Lily's office for a meeting. She dispensed with Anya and introduced me to her daughter, who was going to interpret for me. I do not know what happened to Anya; I was not at all impressed with this, but Lily had caught me on the back foot and so I said nothing. I later felt very uncomfortable and wished I had said something. The dilemma was that, against the 'rule', Lily had hired Anya, rather than allowing me to find my own interpreter, so I assumed she had the right to fire her, if in fact that had happened. Thankfully, this situation only lasted a week, and then I got Anya back again. Apparently she was needed to do some translation for one of the doctors. But why was I not told this?

However, the positive result of the meeting was that I now had some kind of schedule to follow and some direction, which was good, as I felt there was much I would like to do. The question was, how to suggest changes without causing offence.

Now that I was based at Acar, my new schedule involved occasionally staying overnight so I could observe/participate in the community meeting. This was a long and badly organised affair. One meeting did not finish until eleven p.m., having started at seven p.m. Community meetings in general could be tedious but they were a necessary part of community living. The part that upset me most was the public humiliation which some of the patients were put through for seemingly pathetic, inconsequential rule-breaking. For example, one man had not been keeping his 'bed space' tidy. His punishment was to bring some of his clothes to the meeting room and fold them up, whereupon Lily messed them all up and he had to repeat the folding – over and over. Taking responsibility for one's self and one's possessions is a necessary part of recovery, but the humiliation, in my view, did nothing for the patients' self-esteem; nor, I suspect, for the patient's anger management.

On another occasion – youth day, as I recall – we were to stay over and we were joined by a group of journalists invited to marvel at the good work being carried out! They were treated to the excursion around the centre, similar to the one I had had the pleasure of on my first visit there. This was followed by a programme of poetry, music and dancing whilst simultaneously trying to eat. Later we donned our outdoor clothes and went to sit round a bonfire, before the bus took us back into Pavlodar.

Chatting to the journalists on the way back, I found they had not been as impressed with what they had seen as had been intended. They clearly had some concerns as to the management, as obviously did I, and I did not feel sufficiently loyal to defend Lily and her work. My main concern was her relationship to the patients. In my opinion not only did she try to discourage dependency, but her whole demeanour actively encouraged the patients to become totally dependent on her, to the extent that they called her 'mother'. This is such an alien concept to Western beliefs and positively unhelpful to a recovering addict; I cringed every time I watched or heard her talk to the patients.

Sharing skills? Not a concept Lily had ever considered.

Cooking chips

The new flat

Nine

MORE FRUSTRATIONS AND LIGHT RELIEF

I spent a Friday evening with Tom at a nice but overpriced restaurant, followed by watching a video. I decided to stay over at Tom's as finding a taxi late at night was not easy. In the morning we leisurely showered and dressed – well, actually, Tom did the leisurely part; I was ready and waiting for ages! We breakfasted at a great cafe, which set me up for the day.

I had thought Saturday evening was going to be another lonely one, but I was invited to a jamming session/party by one of the American volunteers. I duly followed her directions, becoming slightly more apprehensive the nearer I got. I finally found them in a filthy room behind one of the clubs, but at least everyone was warm and friendly and welcoming. This was mainly due, I realised, to the copious amounts of vodka they had already consumed. Lots of food, drink and cigarettes were shared – some of which we had brought, of course. The music was good, amateur level but great fun. The (Kazakh) band played mostly Western music, which they had all listened to in previous times underground, and whose lyrics they had learned well. So we danced and sang and drank and so on.

As the evening wore on, though, I realised that something other than nicotine and alcohol was being ingested. One girl was completely out of it: she was there physically but unable to speak or move. Should I carry her to the centre? I wondered. As the party decreased in energy and we started to drift away, some of the guys helped her out – and home, I presume.

I decided I did need to be looking for a new apartment. My current one was only intended to be for two months, and after returning from my trip to Semey, I noticed once again that various things had been moved and some removed (not my personal things but, for example, the steamer and a saucepan lid!). I found myself questioning why I felt so affronted by what I saw as an intrusion on my privacy. I do believe it was yet another cultural difference, which was hard to understand but which another Kazakhstani would have no problem with. I had to remind myself that most Kazakhs live in small flats where nobody has any private space at all. Lack of privacy was one compromise I did not want to make. I thought a move was a good option.

I went to see a flat belonging to a friend of one of the American volunteers, but it was very small. It felt particularly small because I had just visited another American volunteer who was 'housesitting' in a beautiful, huge apartment with a washing machine, television and video – lucky girl!

I must remember the positives. I spent a lovely evening with an American girl who was working for a company in Pavlodar. We went to a club, where I met an interesting, but very young, man called Ivan. We met up again a few times. He was lovely, but quite what he wanted with me was unclear – apart from the obvious. I doubted I would see him again. Still, it would have been a pleasant interlude and distraction, especially as, in addition to all the other problems, I had found an odd lump between my ribs, which was rather worrying.

There was still no sign of the snow we were promised, though I had it on good authority from my Russian teacher that it would snow soon. I wondered whether their forecasters came from the same training ground as the British ones. The temperature rarely rose above freezing, but it was quite bearable, especially when accompanied by bright skies and sunshine.

I saw a strange phenomenon in the sky one Saturday night – it was late but I was (relatively) sober. The moon was full, and way beyond and around it there was a huge circle. No-one could explain what it was, but Anya told me it was a frequent occurrence. Then one night, the full moon was orange! The people who set off those nuclear explosions have a lot to answer for.

The work front was changing, but slowly. I was now doing three three-hour 'trainings' a week with the patients. The word 'training' is a bit misleading. My training – as a counsellor – was about helping people find their own solutions, albeit showing them there were other options than the ones they had taken previously. So my work with clients would not be called 'training'. The way the so-called psychotherapists worked was indeed a kind of training, or an enforced change of thinking.

So, for example, my training and practice was to encourage the clients (note, I call them clients, whereas in the centre they were called patients) to express their feelings – about the past and also the present, as a way of finding an alternative way to dealing with uncomfortable feelings, other than the use of drugs or alcohol. This goes somewhat against what they were being taught elsewhere in the centre, whereby they were encouraged to keep busy, not to think about the past and, whatever they did, to control their feelings. I anticipated some confusion for the clients, and my experience told me that controlling one's feelings was not necessarily the best option.

I also started to do a couple of individual sessions – an interesting experience, especially working through an interpreter. The client had to trust not just the counsellor but also the interpreter. If not set up carefully, the client's conversation took place with the interpreter rather than the counsellor. A far from satisfactory arrangement, but I had no choice.

There were many suggestions I wanted to make about the overall treatment that I felt would improve the quality of the treatment, but I was not being asked and approaching the subject was not easy.

However, my preoccupation now was trying to find a new flat. One I saw was owned by a lady who was currently living with and taking care of her mother. All her belongings were in the flat, and as it was very small, it felt quite claustrophobic. Another, also very small flat, had an interesting arrangement whereby the bath was in the kitchen! The third needed a lot of renovation, and my boss made the suggestion I could live out at Acar for the month whilst the work was being carried out. In my opinion this was not even to be considered. So the search continued.

I got the feeling my boss was quite desperate to have me move to Acar, as per her original plan. She did not like to be thwarted. The room at Acar that I had been assigned to use as an office/bedroom was reached by going through another bedroom occupied by three residents, so it was not confidential. The bathroom for the use of the three girls and Anya and I was beyond my room. There was no lock on the door, but I should have been used to a lack of privacy by now, shouldn't I? I was in my room one day, attempting to have a session with a client, when the noise from next door became increasingly intrusive, so I went to ask them to shut up. When I opened the door they (a man and a woman) were sitting in a somewhat compromising position on the bed, giggling and chatting – very appropriate with a confidential session taking place next door.

There was no telephone available to me, no Internet connection, and the only transport was the centre bus – out and back once a day. Also, the kettle that had been very kindly supplied for me had now disappeared, so I could not keep up my surreptitious supply of caffeine! Yes, caffeine was on the black list. It seemed caffeine, like alcohol and drugs, was definitely banned.

So, no, no, no – staying at Acar for a month was not an option. My Russian teacher heard of a suitable flat, which sounded nice. But tragically her sister and brother-in-law and eighteen-month-old niece were killed in a road accident by a nineteen-year-old drunk man. She and her family went to the village for the funerals and did not return until after the flat had gone. So I was back to square one.

The social front was, again, a mixed bag. I had met the two American volunteers, who seemed nice, but only one was a socialite, the other was very quiet and did not fit the stereotype. However, I did go to see *Crime and Punishment* with Sandra, an American volunteer and a Russian friend of hers at the theatre. What a fabulous experience that was! I understood precious little of the dialogue and yet thoroughly enjoyed it – if that's the word to describe watching a very powerful and dynamic play in a language you barely understand. Whether it was the power of Dostoevsky's writing or the acting ability or the direction or a combination of all, it was an emotionally stirring experience.

I went to one of the city's clubs a few times with one or two of the other volunteers, but was left feeling tired and jaded. The club vibrated, not only with the music but with the constant strobes and lasers, leaving my visual and auditory senses somewhat disturbed.

Then, one Saturday night, at about two o'clock in the morning, I was woken by a loud knocking on the door. Needless to say, I was terrified. On asking, in a rather pathetic voice, who was there, I was relieved to recognise the voice of a guy I had met a week or so earlier at the club. Rather against my better judgement, I let him and three of his friends in. They had been to a wedding and wanted somewhere to drink tea, would you believe? So, tea they drank and, in true Kazakh style, I managed to rustle up a snack to accompany it. They were drunk but not at all unpleasant, so it was an amusing little episode. The three friends started to take their leave and it became clear my 'friend' wasn't. I have to say this was not a hard decision to make; because I felt lonely much of the time, I was more than happy to have the company of an attractive young man. Firstly, though, he said he was hungry and wanted some chips. There I did draw the line, but pointed him in the direction of the potatoes, peeler, pan and oil. So, with a towel wrapped around his waist (nothing else, I might add), he proceeded to cook his chips whilst I giggled to myself. So there you have it, an interesting, pleasant but sleepless night.

It was now December. I imagined the hype for Christmas had been building in England and I started to wonder what it would be like here. This being a largely Muslim community, Christmas obviously would not be celebrated, and the orthodox folk celebrated on 7 January. So it could be one long binge from Xmas through to New Year, Old New Year and the orthodox Christmas. I had now bought most of the presents I needed for the family. So I tried to parcel them up in whatever paper I could find – scrap paper, tissue paper and so on. I wrote labels and spent ages packing them up ready to post. Fortunately I had the foresight to ask Anya to accompany me to the post office. Of course there was a form to complete, in duplicate, for each parcel, and then each parcel had to be unwrapped and examined minutely so that all my careful packing was to no avail. I found it very distressing to have all these personal gifts which I had lovingly wrapped torn apart and examined in public. One hour and twenty minutes later the gifts were all re-wrapped and posted, leaving me feeling quite drained. The sad thing was that when my children opened these pathetic little, but nevertheless precious, gifts they would have no idea what angst I had in the buying, wrapping and posting process – how could they?

Umut, my Russian teacher, who had promised to help me find a flat, seemed to have become incommunicado. For two reasons, this was frustrating: I so wanted to be able to speak Russian and I needed help to find a flat. I decided to call one of the other respondents to my advert for a teacher, and see what came of that.

More frustrations at work resulted in a low week all round. There were so many things I wanted to talk to Lily about, but she was never available. Her management of Acar went against my training so much I wanted to scream. Basically she had built up a community whereby she had the power and control and she had her favourites who enjoyed privileges, such as using dope. It created such dissonance and jealousy that the community was not a good place to be. She appeared to be completely unaware of transference and counter-transference issues, or at the very least paid no attention to them. I found it unbelievable as it went against our Western beliefs as to how to run a therapeutic community. Supervision for staff was, of course, an unknown concept.

I finally had an opportunity to challenge her about the dope smokers. She was clearly uncomfortable but said they had all been tested and were negative. How can this be? I asked myself. The owner of the dope had admitted responsibility, but as he was currently on a 'training' in Pavlodar, there was little to be done. When he returned to Acar, he would be watched! I was sure he was shaking in his shoes.

I also had the temerity to ask about staff meetings. When I arrived in the mornings, I had no way of finding out what had happened overnight, what the current atmosphere was like, and it added to my feeling like an outsider just dropping in. Apparently I could always speak to the duty psychologist. I knew I could, but there was no sense of cohesion, of the staff working together, and so certainly no team work. It was like working in a bubble. As far as I could tell there were never any meetings to discuss the residents'/patients' progress or treatment. It was all controlled by Lily. Then she had the gall to tell me how hard it all was, that she could not delegate to anyone. I did not believe she would want to delegate anyway.

It left me feeling very depressed, as we went around in circles and got nowhere. She was not open to any suggestions or offers to help by taking some of the responsibility.

Ten

INTERESTING EXCURSIONS

It was just a couple of weeks before Christmas and it did not feel like it at all, except for the weather. Pavlodar was now a white city and was much improved for that. I still did not know where I would be spending Christmas, but if I stayed in Pavlodar it would be a very different experience from a normal Christmas for me. There were virtually no decorations in the shops, other than a few for their New Year celebrations. The ice blocks had arrived which they would use to build the very famous Pavlodar ice palace. Apparently it was usually a superb spectacle, but as luck would have it they had decided this year not to spend so much and it would be a much-reduced cottage!

So what were the options? Going home was not an option as I had neither the time nor the money. So Tom and I could just stay in Pavlodar. It was, after all, just another day, which was meaningless without friends and family around. Mike let us know he had made plans with his girlfriend. I felt that I just want to crawl into a hole and sulk.

As the winter progressed, my diet became more and more restricted as the only vegetables available were the inevitable cabbage, carrots and beetroot. I was beginning to crave Marmite and hummus. Imagine my excitement, then, when Sandra returned from a trip to Almaty with chickpeas and tahini – the ingredients to make hummus. But what a disappointment! I carefully mashed the chickpeas with a fork and added the tahini, garlic and so on, but it was definitely not up to Waitrose standards. I would just have to try again sometime when I could face the possibility of another let-down.

One morning I got a call from Anya to say we had no work today. I had no idea why, but chose not to question it and so, change of plan! I would go with Tom on a little adventure to which he had invited me earlier but I had declined, expecting to be working.

After a night of not being able to get to sleep, getting up on a cold, grey morning did not come easily. Having checked the thermometer, I knew I needed to dress fairly warmly as it was minus ten today. At least walking on freshly fallen snow which was glistening and sparkling would be a joy.

As I set off for the tram, which was just a few minutes' walk from my apartment, I saw small gangs of women with what looked like homemade shovels trying to clear the snow for the pedestrians. This was a pretty fruitless task, I suspected, as the sky was grey today and looked full of more snow.

I was lucky as the number eight tram arrived immediately. I took a seat and relaxed into my favourite pastime – people watching! Everybody but everybody wore a hat. The men's favourite seemed to be the furry sort, which they wore perched on the top of their heads. Some women also wore furry hats, very stylish and attractive, while others opted for the bog-standard tea-cosy effect, and the old women wrapped thick (usually grey) shawls around their heads and necks and tucked them into their coats. In this temperature there was little to smile about, but when I was treated to a smile the amount of gold to be seen was sometimes shocking and reminded me of Jaws from James Bond. The children had beautifully coloured clothes and looked like miniature Michelin men, they were so well togged up. It was very difficult to see any babies. If they were taken out, they were wrapped in a sort of papoose and often their faces were covered too; this was partly to protect them from the cold but also because one is not allowed to look at some of the Muslim babies.

I arrived at my destination some twenty minutes later, having carefully watched the stops, as well as the people, as it was easy to miss your stop unless alert. I walked the few hundred yards to Tom's office. His NGO set up and supported other NGOs. It was a small office on the ground floor of the inevitable apartment block. The staff members were just arriving and we sat in the kitchen and drank tea whilst we waited for the transport to arrive.

After a while, Tom, Anya (my interpreter), Rosaly (the community development worker) and I boarded the minibus and set off for the village (the name of which sounded like Sharaganak), which was about fifty kilometres away. The steppe looked infinitely more attractive covered in snow. However, the condensation inside and the mud splashes on the outside prevented me from seeing too much.

We discussed how we were to conduct the meeting. As far as we were aware, we were to meet a group of women in this village who were setting up a self-help group. Quite why we were going was not too clear, but this was quite normal here! We decided to tell them a little about ourselves. Tom would talk about the different types of self-help groups in England and I would talk about the groups I had been involved in. We were keen to involve the women and so we planned a participatory exercise for them.

We lapsed into silence and enjoyed the comfort of the minibus, so different from the Acar one, which rattled and banged and had no heater. Eventually we arrived at the village, but it seemed it was not the one where the group was to be set up. We were taken into a school and introduced to a teacher who took us to her class to talk to her pupils. They were mostly very shy but curious, and some struggled to introduce themselves. They were aged between ten and eleven and had been learning English for only two months.

After we chatted to them, we were taken on an excursion around the school. There were one hundred and seventy pupils, but maybe ten years ago there had been more than a thousand. People were leaving the villages in search of work, and they were concerned that village life was deteriorating. The building was quite old, with wooden floors and basic equipment, but a nice atmosphere. We were shown the history room, the biology room and the library, and we talked to a small group of slightly older pupils. We were also introduced to one or two other people, whose names I cannot remember but who had some interest in the self-help group.

Tom took over the talking, and I took the opportunity to ask to visit the toilet. My guide and I donned our outdoor gear again and set off down two flights of stairs and then outside. Around the side of the building was a small outhouse with two toilets. The doors did not fit and the wind whistled through. The toilet was a simple affair: a hole in the ground and no more. I was worried I would drop my camera, which I had forgotten to leave behind, and also that I may spoil my (very expensive) *dublonka* – a big furry coat. I completed my task and believed I probably had frostbite in my *derriere*.

We returned to find lunch was served for us. Despite telling them I am a vegetarian, we were served *beşbarmaq* – a traditional Kazakh dish with lovely fatty mutton floating in an equally greasy sauce, with a sort of pasta underneath (it looked very white and my brain told me it was also fat). There was no way I could eat the dish, so I made do with the fresh, warm bread and a salad of tomatoes, peppers, gherkins and cucumbers cut up small and marinated in an oily, vinegary sauce – it was quite tasty. To follow, we had biscuits, chocolates and tea, lots of tea. The Kazakhs are as fanatical about their tea as we are! However, they brew the tea in a small teapot, with just enough water to soak the leaves, and then pour a little into each cup and top up with hot water – an interesting variation.

Following lunch, we boarded the bus and set off to the next village, seven kilometres away. There, we were taken to a ramshackle building which had been donated to this self-help group and it was explained that they would all help to renovate this building and they expected to have it ready for the 'grand opening' on 12 December (I very much doubted this). Then we went to the small school building, which had two classrooms and was bright and warm. It transpired that this was where we were to meet the ladies.

All six ladies arrived, seeming bemused, and they asked us questions about us. For example:

'Where is your family?'

'How many children do you have?'

'How old are they?'

'Where is your husband?'

The latter was one of the trickiest to answer, as divorce is still not common in Kazakhstan and I was feeling too vulnerable to be judged on this one.

'So, why are you here in Kazakhstan when you have family in England?'

I attempted to explain: 'Well, my children are all grown-up and independent, and they don't need me to look after them anymore.' This probably cut no ice here, where children tended to live with their parents even after they married.

The conversation was a three-way one. The ladies talked in Kazakh, our guide (the teacher from the first school) translated into Russian but also liked to put in her own two-pence-worth and Anya translated the

Russian into English. It became quite unmanageable as the women tried to speak all at once and were not used to having to wait for translations.

Anyway, we chatted, abandoning our plan and just going with the flow; it was the only thing we could do. We departed maybe an hour and a half later and they wanted to show us the bakery, but it was closed, and in trying to turn around, the van got well and truly stuck in the snow. We climbed out to help push it and found ourselves knee-deep in a snowdrift and we could not budge the van one centimetre. We borrowed shovels and, after an age and now beginning to feel very cold, we dug ourselves out and eventually we set off back to Pavlodar.

The next day, my Russian teacher, Umut, resurfaced and we met to view yet another apartment. The location was good, much nearer the town, but it was not attractive and so another one bit the dust. Only went to confirm my hunch I would be in the apartment for the year in the end!

On the way out we heard the most pathetic noise. The landing was in darkness so I extracted my mini torch and looked for the source of the noise. It was a tiny kitten, huddled in the corner by the lift. It was so young it could not walk and it was making the most awful sound; it was heart-wrenching. Umut insisted we left it and would not allow me to touch it even. It was truly heart-breaking, but believing there was no RSPCA equivalent in Kazakhstan, I thought I had no choice. So I walked away, feeling very upset, only to find later there was some kind of animal refuge. At least I knew what to do in the future.

The next morning, having been to the club the evening before, I was looking forward to a nice lie-in with nothing to do other than relax. I found myself wishing there was someone here with whom I could spend the day. I followed my usual strategy of keeping busy: I showered, dressed and finished off the week's washing (at least my wrist could now cope with wringing the washing) and last night's washing up, and then decided to try some retail therapy. So off I went to my favourite shopping place.

There are very few single shops in Pavlodar; mostly they are grouped together in one building, which obviously saves on the heating and makes for more comfortable shopping. I tried on numerous pairs of jeans and eventually found a pair which the girl assured me were *xoroshor* (good). I bought them but with some misgivings as they were so tight that if I were to put on an ounce I would not be able to get them on!

I still felt the need to be cheered up, so I also decided to be brave and try a hairdresser's. I reckoned it did not really matter what she did as long as she did not scalp me. It was not a bad job and cost me all of one pound twenty-five. What is more, not a single hair slipped under my clothes. This was due to a sort of paper collar which she wound around my neck before putting on the gown and then folding the collar over – very effective.

I then bought a jumper. It was not really big enough, but who cared? I liked the colour and it would be a change from the ones I'd worn to the point of complete boredom.

I got the tram home, whilst musing on the fact that when I did not know exactly where the stop was, as there were no signs, I just had to look out for the cigarette ends and the discarded husks from the sunflower seeds. These were sold at the roadside from bags or boxes or small pots – usually straight into a pocket. There was clearly an art to eating these seeds and spitting out the husks without using one's hands, which I had never mastered nor particularly wished to, to be honest.

Of course the husks were not the only debris on the ground –Kazakhs, being mostly Asian like to clear both their sinuses and lungs from time to time in that somewhat unattractive method which does not involve a handkerchief. Spoils the whiteness of the snow!

A few days later was the second Independence Day holiday, but I was supposed to be working. Tom had not realised I was working and had arranged for me to accompany him and his Russian teacher and her group of Scouts to a village where they were to sledge and ski and generally frolic. I was hugely disappointed not to be able to go. And then, the gods must have been on my side after all. At half past seven in the morning Anya rang to tell me we did not have to go in after all! So I made a quick call to Tom to ask them to wait for me, and off I set.

I met Tom, Jenna and something like forty Scouts (mostly girls) at the bus station. We boarded the bus, and half an hour later arrived in a little village. We walked through to the woods where we set up camp, raising the flag on a tree and chanting some kind of Scout song. We were then commissioned to gather wood for a fire, a sensible task as it was more than freezing at minus eighteen and we needed to keep moving to keep warm. We left the lads to light the fire and get some water to boil while we went off to find sledges, and we spent a while careering down the slopes, screaming and usually ending by falling off into the snow. When the water had boiled we had a shared picnic and hot tea, which was very welcome.

A game was set up then on the frozen river. It was like rugby, using a piece of rolled-up vinyl as a ball and with fewer rules. We declined to join in; it looked somewhat rough and of course, being genteel English, that was not quite our thing. Actually having broken my arm I found I was now much less confident of such capers than I was. However that did not stop me having a go at skiing. Forget Klosters! Think small, gentle slopes. But nevertheless it was good fun and I survived it without breaking anything other than the rather flimsy ski.

More songs and chants followed as the flag was lowered, and then we set off back for the bus, looking forward (well, speaking for myself) to a nice hot bath. A good day all in all!

It was finished off by going to a concert, the venue for which was reminiscent of an old jazz club – very dark and smoky. The music ranged from awful to quite haunting. It made a nice change from sitting in my lonely room

Writing my diary in our room in Zhabagly

Our walk on Christmas day

A farmer in Zhabagly

Ponies grazing in Zhabagly – Christmas Day

Tom and me – Christmas Day

Eleven

A VERY STRANGE CHRISTMAS

I finally understood the reason I was here – out of my comfort zone. It was to work on my impatience and my need to be in control, in terms of needing to know what was happening. It was beginning to feel that both were being severely put to the test every single day.

Tom and I had decided we would go away for the Christmas period, but I spent a week trying to contact Tom to make arrangements, to no avail. This tested me sorely. Then one day (not the first) the bus failed to pick me up for work. I waited for over half an hour with the temperature at minus eighteen before finally going home again. As luck would have it the phone rang five minutes later and it was my son, to whom I had not spoken for months. It was so lovely to hear his voice, and we spent the first few minutes laughing and crying. He had tried to call many times and could never get through, so having just got home from a party, at three a.m., he decided he would try again. He also said that, reading between the lines, it sounded like life was very difficult. 'Why not come home?' he said. Why not indeed?

Well, we had Christmas to get through first. After much hassle, both in getting some kind of response from Tom and in getting tickets, we finally took the train via Semey down to Almaty – a slightly shorter distance this way, so twenty-eight hours only. Mind you, the scenery was the same wherever I looked, so I decided it was best to lose myself in a good book.

Until, that is, the compartment door was opened and a third companion joined us. Though non-English speaking, his actions, in leaping off to buy a bottle of vodka and sharing his little bits of food, were clear. So we shared food and vodka and started to become very friendly. His son's name was Timor, like Tom, and Tom said he reminded him of his father. Oh dear, this was going to be an interesting journey.

Then he said it was time to go off to find his friends in the next carriage, who also had vodka and lots of food and were very happy to share with us. So we toddled along to find these friends, and indeed they did have copious amounts of vodka and food with which we were generously plied. Eventually I realised if I didn't make a move, I may not find our compartment ever again, so we wobbled off and fell asleep for several hours. When we awoke we found we had been covered with blankets and tucked in!

Our new friend was very insistent that we call him when we arrived home and visit him and his family. This would be difficult because of the language, but we would give it a go, we said.

Arriving in Almaty was stressful. We, and any other foreign looking passengers who wanted a taxi (and even those who didn't), were hassled by the taxi drivers and their touts. It was a nightmare. They were all charging far too much and, despite being able to barter a little, we ended up paying far in excess of what we knew was the norm; we were worn down in the end.

We went to the apartment of three girls, two of whom worked at the NGO with Tom when he first arrived and then came to Almaty to seek their fame and fortune – a bit like Dick Whittington. As neither of them had found jobs yet, they were very cramped in a one-room place, but they said we were welcome to use their bathroom, and did I ever need a good scrub after being on the train.

Almaty was looking beautiful with lots of frozen snow covering the trees – so pretty. Later that day we took the train down to Aksu-Zhabagly. There were no compartments free so we had to go *Plascart*, and I refuse to travel that way EVER again. It was like an open carriage, with people sleeping in two or even three tiers – it is difficult to describe but I had never felt so uncomfortable in a travelling situation before. On top of this, the carriage was cold and very dimly lit. There was not enough hot water, and so the soup-in-a-cup I had bought and really fancied was not to be.

There was also a lot of drunkenness. One guy sort of lurched onto me, but fortunately the guy above with whom we had conversed earlier slid down and stood between this guy and me, and when the Big Fat Railway Controller arrived, he sloped off. It seemed to me even the guards, railway police *et al.* made the most of these train rides to get completely rat-arsed. So feigning sleep was a good strategy, I decided, and sure enough I did fall asleep and, as far as I know, was left alone. On reflection it was the only feasible strategy as the light was too dim to read and it was too cold to do anything other than wrap up in the blankets.

So it was that early on Christmas morning we found ourselves in Aksu-Zhabagly, which was so achingly beautiful and such a contrast to the awful train. Zhabagly is a small, sprawling village with the end of the Tien Shan mountains on one side and the Black Mountains on the other.

We were met by our guide, Svetlana, and taken to our 'homestay', an extension of a person's house used for tourists. Firstly not a tenement block in sight! All single-storey dwellings, mostly with their own few sheep, cows, horses – all very simple and basic.

Our accommodation had four bedrooms, a bathroom, a toilet and a dining/sitting room with the traditional low tables and fantastic rugs hanging everywhere. It was all very comfortable and we were made to feel very welcome. However, we were not warm and I was not feeling too well.

The food was copious but I could not do it justice. I managed to eat the two fried eggs as I knew we would be hiking over the mountains and I would need some energy. These eggs reminded me of my childhood and visits to my uncle's farm, where we would have fresh farm eggs. The eggs were followed by wild-cherry jam, doughnuts and tea.

After a little rest we set off into the mountains. It was so beautifully bright and sunny, with a clear blue sky – fantastic and just what we needed to take our minds off family and friends at home, eating, drinking and making merry!

We made our way to the ranger's house, built with money from a grant. It was quite spacious and in a wonderful spot at the top of a gorge. There was no furniture, just simple mats and rugs. Svetlana had brought with her a concoction of traditional tea and berries, which was delicious. Then we slowly wound our way down again.

After lunch we took to the horses, following some mad Kazakh fellow who kept grabbing my horse's reigns even though he was perfectly well behaved. It was a nice, gentle ramble, over hills and across streams, but we did not realise just how cold we were until we stopped. Again the scenery was beautiful, but we were so frozen that we did not object to being brought back twenty-five minutes early.

We had been promised a banya when we got back and I could not wait to get into the hot water and steam. However, I had to curb my impatience as the banya was not ready, so we just shivered for a while until tea arrived (for 'tea' read cakes, sweets, fruit and biscuits). The banya was worth the wait. As mentioned before, it is the traditional way of bathing. There is often a village one to be heated up and used once a week, but many people have their own now in the villages and in their *dachas*. Basically it's a combination of tipping bowls of lovely hot water over you as a preliminary to washing, repeating to rinse, and then sitting and enjoying the steam, using more hot/cold water as you wish. Just the job: it certainly defrosted me!

So that was Christmas Day – well, not quite! I had made sure the family had my mobile number so we could speak on this auspicious day. However, I had overlooked the fact that several thousand acres of steppe were between us and civilisation, and so there was a very spasmodic and weak signal; hence no connection. I tried to call out from the house phone but they had an infuriating habit of putting some block on the phones so you could only make local calls. My warm serenity was on the verge of disappearing. Eventually I managed, on a fleeting two-bar signal, to get an SMS to my daughter, and later they managed to get through to me. What a relief – not talking to any family on Christmas Day had definitely not been on my agenda.

On Boxing Day we had another ramble over the mountains, up what Svetlana called a gorge; in all honesty it was just a little stream, but nevertheless it was very beautiful. Svetlana was a great fount of information and I learned a lot from her about the deprivation and struggle that the Kazakhs went through after the breakdown of the USSR. There had been little or no infrastructure and it took three or four years for it to be built up. Food queues were common, jobs few and far between, and life was grim. I had had no idea just how bad it had been and felt quite ashamed of my ignorance.

So that was our little sojourn to Zhabagly, and sadly we had to set off on our return trip. Despite the wonderful scenery and accommodation, it had all been a little marred by the fact that I was not feeling too well: I had flu-like symptoms and a cough. So I was planning a good sleep on the train. Then a very nice-looking young couple joined us in our compartment. They had been to his sister's wedding and were returning home to Almaty where he was a medical student and she was a law student. They were clearly well oiled already, but the inevitable vodka was produced and large amounts were quickly consumed – not by me, obviously.

The first problem occurred when I went to have cigarette in the little area at the back of the carriage. The guy followed me and tried to drag me into another compartment and then into the disgusting toilet (no mistaking his intention, unfortunately). I managed to break away and get back to our compartment, but before I could explain to Tom what had just happened, Tom chose that moment to go and have a cigarette himself and the girl went with him.

Without any further ado, our friend lurched at me and fell on top of me – quite revolting, but at least he was nice-looking, just very drunk! I doubt he was capable of actually doing anything anyway, but then nature intervened: he went very pale and disappeared (but as the toilet was next to us I knew exactly where he had been and what he had been doing).

When he returned he was stripped to his underpants and he indicated that once his girlfriend and Tom had gone to sleep he would join me. Fortunately his stomach had other ideas and off he trotted about five more times, before finally collapsing on his bunk, still heaving, and then quickly starting to snore so some kind of peace reigned. Whilst he snored, the 'girlfriend' called her 'real' boyfriend, and Tom and I finally got some sleep.

We then had a day in Almaty, before the train departed for Pavlodar. I had been in touch with a friend of my son's, who was deputy director of the British Council in Almaty. What a great chap he is; I really enjoy his company every time I meet him. I thought I might ask to adopt him whist we were out in Kazakhstan! Anyway his hospitality was great – lovely fresh towels and breakfast, just the job to scrub the memory of our drunken friend. Sadly, though, he also told us of the news just breaking from the Indian Ocean – the awful death toll caused by the tsunami. Being in a country like Kazakhstan, and in a city like Pavlodar with no TV and no radio, I felt very cut off, and hearing this news exacerbated that feeling of being out of touch with the rest of the world. To be honest it had become a matter of sheer survival and it was not until something like the tsunami happened that I was shaken out of that 'pure survival' mode.

So we had a lovely day with my son's friend and a few other acquaintances in Almaty before the final haul back to Pavlodar – only thirty-three hours and this time no real problems, except I really felt unwell and basically just slept most of the way.

On my return it was made obvious that my removal from the apartment was more urgent – especially after I refused to let my landlady sleep on the sofa! Was I such a heartless bitch or was that request really inappropriate? I was now wondering what the norm was. Whatever, my boss had arranged for me to view another flat, which was fine. It was clean, although small and not very warm, and even further out of the city, at the end of the tram line. Anyway it seemed I had little choice, so I would move in on the thirtieth – supposedly for one month, whilst the flat I had seen weeks ago was renovated.

A few days before New Year's Eve, Tom's organisation was going to a hotel a few miles away for a 'playaway', to which they had kindly invited me too. The problem, as always, was not being able to join in the chatter, which left me feeling excluded and obviously frustrated. However, when 'Santa Claus' arrived it was better, as he organised silly games for us to play. I was quite happy to play the games, as it was a good distraction from sitting around a dinner table feeling as if I were invisible. My self-esteem was not helped, however, when later we retired to our rooms and one of the girls with whom I was sharing clearly liked an audience when undressing. She was so beautiful, with such a great body, that I turned over and groaned before going to sleep.

The next morning, sledging and skating were on offer and I saw that it was a beautiful place. The weather was cold but bright and sunny. But I was feeling wretched, and much as I wanted to join in the fun, I did not have the energy. I just wanted to curl up in bed.

I arrived home to find Anya and a guy waiting to move me to the new flat. They had brought an old hospital van for my stuff with a driver who clearly wished he were far away. Nobody knew exactly where the flat was and so we drove round for ages before finally finding what we thought was the entrance, and we unloaded my stuff – only to find it was the wrong entrance. So we ferried my stuff over to another entrance and lugged it up the eight floors to my new abode. The driver and Anya beat a hasty retreat, and I was left in the remote place, not even sure where it was, without knowing a soul, on 30 December and feeling so ill – and not a little sorry for myself.

New Year's Eve was a non-event. Neither Tom nor I felt like going to the club, so Tom insisted I went to his flat where we watched a DVD. Later we wandered into town to find there was nothing going on, looked at the few pathetic ice statues, wished each other a Happy New Year and then went back to his where we went to bed.

Farewell 2004.

Twelve

TIME TO REVIEW

Not a very auspicious start to 2005: waking up in Tom's messy flat where there was no juice, no tea, no coffee, basically no nothing. So I dragged myself off to try to buy some things, only to find everywhere was shut. I made my miserable way back to my lonely, cold flat.

The next day we were back to work, out at Acar. The New Year 'programme' which the patients had planned to put on naturally did not start on time, so a lot of time was spent hanging around aimlessly. Once it started, it was quite interesting, with songs and sketches and the like.

The bus to take us home was late leaving, and I had been told that as my flat was so far out of town the work bus would not take me home, so I had to take a bus from the centre out to my flat. In the mornings I had to take a bus to the centre to wait for the Acar bus. I was not happy about this.

The next day, I was feeling thoroughly unwell. Despite it being a public holiday, I felt so wretched I decided I had to see a doctor and get some antibiotics PDQ. The hunt began. No-one seemed to know how to find one. My interpreter was useless when it came to things like this as she was so young, with no life experience, and so I could not count on her at all. In the end I did find a doctor, who diagnosed bronchitis and put me on three lots of pills, and so I was patiently waiting to bounce back to health and, please God, more *joie de vivre*. I was told to stay in for a few days, which suited me fine. *In fact,* I thought, *please can I stay in until the summer?* I think I expended so much energy keeping warm and keeping going, it was draining. I felt pretty dead from the neck down.

Stir Crazy in Kazakhstan

I spent a miserable week or so feeling very sorry for myself because I felt so ill, was so far away from home, my family and friends and was out of touch with the few contacts I had in Pavlodar. What was more, I was in a flat where I knew no-one, it was cold and I had few creature comforts around me. I had hardly any food in and was too ill to go in search of any, and of course no-one called in. In fact it was pretty damn bleak.

But apparently things had to get even worse before they got better. I woke up one morning looking like a monster from hell – I even frightened myself when I looked, albeit cautiously, in the mirror. As it happened, my new Russian teacher was due that morning. Now, how to let her in without frightening her away with one glance at my poor, distended face? I tied a scarf around my face while I endeavoured to explain to her that I need to see a doctor again.

It was clearly an allergy, and I was told it was an allergy to the cold. Well, there is an irony if ever there was one! Still, I was not convinced the diagnosis was correct. Anyhow the antihistamine injections and tablets did the trick, and so I waited in my cold flat, with the temperature hovering at around minus twenty to minus twenty-five, for the next attack.

As soon as the swelling subsided sufficiently I made my way to the post office to pick up a parcel. I had to ask Anya to meet me there as she had my passport (for some reason which escapes me at the moment) and this identification was required before they would hand over the precious parcel. Attempting this when I was still far from well was definitely not a good move. I waited for ages to be served, and then the girl looked as if she was going for lunch. That was the final straw, and I am ashamed to say I embarrassed poor Anya hugely with my angry volley of abuse at the girl, the post office and probably all of Kazakhstan as well!

Once I was up and about a little more, I found there was a slight improvement in the social scene. I went to see a couple of bands live, to the theatre, and to a birthday lunch for a girl who worked at one of the 'universities' – my first visit to a local Kazakh's house in all of the four and a half months I had been there. She seemed quite appalled when I mentioned this fact; she could not understand why that was. She should have asked my erstwhile colleagues, my interpreter, my boss, my neighbours, none of whom had have ever shown me the slightest bit of hospitality.

One Saturday I went with Tom and one of the American volunteers to visit a local artist in his studio. After three bottles of wine and a bottle of cognac, we were all very good friends! His work was amazing and so prolific, in many different styles reflecting his life. We were treated to a personal history of just a fraction of the artworks, in between eating and drinking. Seven hours later we took our leave, with all our senses, well and truly fed.

The month in my new, supposedly temporary, apartment was up at the end of January. When I was told the other one was still not ready and asked whether I would like to stay where I was, I very politely but assertively said, *'HIET!'* (NO!) The trouble was, no-one was doing anything to help me find anything else. So I decided to take Ludmilla's flat (which I had rather stupidly turned down before). Ludmilla was an English teacher who was living with her sick and elderly mother, so her own place was vacant. It was very small, just a sitting room with a bed settee, a kitchen, and a bathroom, but it was very, very warm and very 'well appointed', I think would be an estate agent's description. It was also much nearer the town centre so I felt happy there. The other good point was that it faced west and the setting sun could be very beautiful.

My pre-review of my placement report was due and it was causing me early-morning awakenings. My dilemma was that including everything that was causing me problems was going to alienate Lily even more. So I decided to write it all down for myself, and then decide what to put in the report. I wrote:

> *Lily is totally inaccessible. She has never asked for a meeting with me. When I do manage to track her down, there are constant interruptions – other people coming in to speak with her, the telephone going regularly. Consequently I feel as if I am being a nuisance and am in the way. Plans are never discussed or reviewed. I am still unclear as to what she wants or expects of me. I feel completely devalued and a waste of space. She has done nothing to ensure I have a suitable apartment…*

Enough, no more. I filled an A4 page with my ramblings and it did not look good. How much of this could I say to her without either becoming very angry or crying? How come I had slipped into victim mode so easily? How much more could I have done? What should I do now?

The review, with an officer from the voluntary organisation, took place. I tried to explain my problems and frustrations in as calm a way as possible. In short, I explained that I was not being 'utilised' in the way I had imagined, that I had no sense of job satisfaction, that my boss and I never seemed to be able to have any uninterrupted time to talk and clarify, and that all this was the case after over four months: not good, and I was far from happy.

The next session was between Lily and the volunteer officer, during which she probably talked about her disappointment with me! Finally we all got together. My boss had apparently been waiting for me to suggest what I should be working on. So that was how it worked, but was I telepathic?

Having supposedly cleared the air, I then asked whether my boss and I could meet to set objectives and then meet weekly to review (knowing full well weekly meetings were highly unlikely but might work out at monthly). This was agreed. Oozing charm from every pore, Lily also said I was to tell her of any problems, as she had not known, for example, that I had been ill, or that I had had to cancel my Russian lessons as I now got home too late. These were complete lies, as she did know. How did she get away with it? Because she was a powerful lady and very charming and nobody dared confront her. I had tried to confront her in the past and it had made no difference.

I guessed I just had to draw a line under the past and start a new chapter with her. I had not realised just how optimistic I can be. Did I really think things were going to change?

Then Lily took a new tack. I suspected she might feel a tiny bit guilty, but she displaced her guilt onto Anya (my interpreter), whom she said she had doubts about. Well, I had doubts too, but they did not amount to sacking her, which was what Lily wanted to do. In the beginning, despite the organisation's recommendation that the volunteer employ their own interpreter, the centre, i.e. Lily, had hired Anya. Thus when I arrived I was presented with this lovely, young, inexperienced and, as Anya herself later told me, anorexic, girl. But in the grand scheme of things, she had been the least of my problems. She certainly had not been the support, let alone friend, that I had hoped for, but now Lily had decided Anya did not fit in. Now I think about it, I wonder whether jealousy was the key? The patients were very clearly attracted to Anya, which did not fit in with Lily's total power trip. Whatever the reason, it seemed I had no control over the decision and poor Anya was to be sent on her way. This lack of control over matters that closely affected me was unbelievably frustrating.

Lily then went off to Almaty for a week, so of course nothing was done – as far as I knew. Anya certainly knew nothing, so as usual it was another fine mess. I hoped it would all be forgotten about.

And now from the absurd to the ridiculous! Hard physical exercise has always been a good way to work off frustration and stress for me. So I took myself off to an aerobics class, delivered in Russian of course. It was great fun! It was like going back to the classes I went to in the '80s, which I always enjoyed. Fortunately the fact I understood little of what the teacher said mattered little – I could follow easily enough and knew my numbers sufficiently well to anticipate the next move. It was a really good antidote to all the frustrations and cold as I actually got a sweat on! One girl started to talk to me as we waited for the class to start – she was teaching herself English and, to my shame, she spoke far better English than I do Russian (in my defence, I had not had a lesson in weeks).

The next Saturday I was due to go, with another six colleagues, including Lily, to Aktau, about as far west as you can go in Kazakhstan. It would take fifty-one hours to get there on the train. *Lovely!* I thought. *Please let all the drunks stay away from my compartment!*

I was to deliver a kind of family programme for the families of the addicts in Aktau (basically to support the families and prepare them for the addicts' return). Well, I could but try, and this was the sort of work I had hoped to be doing but had been unable to instigate in Pavlodar. It was not exactly an alien concept, but as the patients came from all over this huge country, the logistics of getting a number of parents together for a few days were well-nigh impossible. The mother/son link was very strong, so I thought the concept of 'detaching with love' was going to be a bigger challenge even than I was used to.

On the way back we would pass through Astana and it so happened my mate Mike was training some social workers there. So I decided I would stop off there and combine a session with them on family dynamics with a social visit with Mike

By the time I was to get back to Pavlodar I would have been in Kazakhstan for five months, and another month should see the start of the thaw.

Train stop on the way to Aktau

Our bus in Aktau

Ice formation, Caspian Sea

Touching the sheep, for luck

Parliament buildings, Astana

Thirteen

THE TRIP TO AKTAU

Can you imagine spending three whole days and two whole nights on a Soviet train with another seven people, only one of whom speaks English and who gets tired of translating? All I can say is I was very glad I had a good book and my diary with me.

As is the norm, the train had scheduled stops along the way and the timetable stuck up on the wall told us exactly how long we had at each station. What is more, the schedule was adhered to and the train was never late (British Rail, eat your heart out!). At one of these stops, when we could purchase food and drink from the very noisy stall holders on the platforms, two of our party were slightly late re-embarking. Realising the train was starting to move, they jumped on further down the train so as not to miss it altogether. They then had to walk up the train to our compartment, but I guess they had not bargained for the ensuing row which followed when they were questioned as to why they had done this, and of course they had to complete a form, putting it all in writing. I tell you it made me think very carefully before disembarking at the next stations, and I am not easily frightened!

This said, the next high spot was when yet another member of our group failed to reach his carriage as the train was pulling out and, despite the attendant seeing him running, he was left behind (with no money)! An almighty row ensued between my boss, Lily, and the attendant. How entertaining that was! Lily was not one to cross. It was all sorted out eventually, thanks to mobile phones. The abandoned member of the group caught the goods train and arrived about eight hours after we did, still clutching the bag of cakes which he had gone to purchase in the first place!

In order to sustain us on this trip, vast quantities of food had been brought along, and even after only twelve hours I was heartily sick of the sight of the grey-coloured chicken and God knows how many dozen hard-boiled eggs being served up – it was a wonder they did not all get salmonella, not that it was that warm on the train.

The only way really to survive these journeys, I found, was moderate quantities of alcohol and sleep. Of course alcohol was not on the menu, as we had two patients with us, but it would have helped enormously. Mind you, Lily had her own way of keeping herself amused – she took along her own private lap dog in the form of a former patient, Billy, the one who could earn a degree in carrying her bags with enormous aplomb and no hint of embarrassment. For some reason Lily seemed to need assistance when visiting the 'bathroom' – well, the stinky toilet. Maybe he held a lavender-scented hankie to her nose? I wondered where I could find a Billy.

As for the facilities on board, there was constant hot water from the *samovar*, but as for the toilets – the less said, the better. I was reminded of holidays in France many years ago when we used to grade campsite toilets. Kazakh trains were definitely of the 'instant constipation' variety! Despite the best efforts of the carriage attendant to keep them clean, the men just seemed inherently incapable of aiming straight!

One of the stops was for three hours in some godforsaken place. We stepped out of the train at ten p.m. into unbelievable cold – at least minus thirty. The station hall had a very high ceiling and candelabras and a double staircase sweeping up to… nothing! We walked through and out the other side and stepped onto what was effectively a huge ice rink. The first cabin we tried smelled of unsavoury food, and we were directed to a slightly larger cafe across the ice rink. It seemed no one else wanted food; they must have been stuffed with grey chicken and hard-boiled eggs. There was no meatless food, so I ordered a salad – not quite what I had in mind, which had been egg, beans and chips, but it was quite tasty – and a cup of tea. Too late to say 'no milk or sugar', so I drink the sweet (evaporated) milky tea. Then the inevitable photos were taken, by the other volunteers, (there must be at least a hundred so far and we were not even halfway there.) I later realised this was probably the first trip/holiday any of them had ever taken, and they were quite charmingly childlike in their excitement and anticipation.

Next door was a shop, and I sought supplies of chocolate and such like, but there was a smell of rotting meat so I needed to leave. I tripped daintily across the ice rink, back into the station, and when the others arrived I was reprimanded for not telling them where I had gone. Where else was I going to go when it is thirty below freezing and there was no alternative welcoming light in sight?

Another stop, and this time a relative of one of our group met us with some hot food. I was persuaded to eat the pasta-type food once they had fished the meat out, and indeed it was quite tasty, despite the lingering flavour of horse!

We woke up the next morning to NO SNOW! I realised I had forgotten what earth looked like. Otherwise, there was nothing to see except a few horses and some frolicking camels.

The endless views of the steppe finally came to an end and we arrived in Aktau. It is an area rich in uranium and oil. I was relieved to hear their Chernobyl plant had closed down. Apparently the oil reserves under the Caspian Sea are the richest in the world and have not been tapped yet. The Kazakh president, in his wisdom, sold all rights to foreigners, presumably to make some fast bucks, and consequently Aktau has quite a large expatriot population and definitely a more prosperous feel to it. None – well, few – of the elderly Ladas and Skodas here, my dear.

We were met by a variety of people and treated like VIPs, although our accommodation in a student hostel was hardly 5*. We four women were in one room and the four guys were next door. The bathing facilities were not good (I will not go into detail, but they were verging on the 'instant constipation' variety), but the beds were clean and comfortable. Copious amounts of food were laid out – mostly meat and, I suspected, horse to boot, but there was also bread and cheese and some of the doughnut-type rolls they like too.

We were told before carrying out any other business, that we were expected at the local television studios the next morning, and so we toddled off to bed. Eight o'clock the next morning saw us all tarting ourselves up. A hairdresser had been sent for Lily – I think she thought she was going on *Dallas*! And off we went.

Now, the population of Aktau is largely Kazakh-speaking and the programme was to be conducted in Kazakh. The problem was that only one of our party could speak Kazakh. So the next hour was spent working out a solution to this problem: Lily was interviewed by herself and we were all to return that evening for round two.

Our next port of call was a small town just a hundred miles away where there was apparently a huge drug problem. *Is there not a big problem in Aktau and is that not why we came?* I asked myself. *And please why, after more than fifty hours travelling, do we have drive another hundred miles? Why oh why?*

Anya, meanwhile, seemed shell-shocked. This was the first time she had been out of Pavlodar, and the realisation was just hitting her that she was to interpret on live television! Poor girl.

Our transport was a '50s-type bus and it was a bit rickety but got us there with no problems. It was quite interesting to see a change of scenery – it reminded me of the moonscape scenery of Lanzarote – and of course it was much milder here than in Pavlodar, just above freezing.

We had lunch in a restaurant, by which time we had picked up four ladies whom, silly me, I thought might be some of the mothers I was supposed to be working with. Wrong – one was the director of a school (she spoke French so she and I communicated badly in French while everyone else looked on, bemused) and the others, I think, were businesswomen. After lunch we were asked – nay, pushed – onto the dance floor. At this point I decided there had been a terrible mistake: wires must have been crossed and they thought we were a dance troupe, as certainly no addicts or families had appeared. The four of us somewhat self-consciously danced for a few minutes.

After this bizarre episode, we boarded our charabanc and were taken to a school where the others were to give a talk on the evils of taking drugs and the benefits of our treatment centre. Another ride, another school, another talk, but still none of the mothers whom our organiser had told me were waiting to see me. Later Lily said she had invited them to join the group waiting for me in Aktau. Of course they were going to travel the hundred miles. Needless to say, they did not.

So back to the TV centre. I now had a Kazakh interpreter and our Kazakh speaker would do most of the rest of the talking. Then it turned out there was also a small audience of young people, plus a phone-in! I had no clue what was being discussed, and when I was asked a question, none of my colleagues knew what I was saying as they didn't speak either English or the Kazakh into which I was translated. All good fun. Such good fun they decided they had to do a repeat performance on the Saturday, but in Russian this time.

Wednesday was the big day, then, when I was to work with a group of twenty mothers as arranged by our esteemed organiser. When I walked in, highly prepared with warm-up exercises, worksheets, role plays and so on, there were no jostling hordes of parents, just two, very anxious-looking people there. Gradually over the course of the morning another twelve turned up – each time of course chairs had to be found, and introductions and explanations made. The local organiser (the mother of one of our patients) was probably in the most need of some help, in my humble opinion, but she drifted in at one point, talked over me, made telephone calls in a loud voice on her mobile and then left.

On another occasion a doctor walked into the room, escorting a patient. The patient (and probably the doctor too) was clearly confused – agitated, he threatened to kill his mother as she was so controlling. I tried to talk to him and calm him down, noting the fear in the eyes of the others in the group. I promised him he could speak to Lily later to arrange his treatment and he eventually left. Great material for discussion with the families!

Each subsequent day we had fewer people, but those who did stay took up my suggestion of setting up a self-help group. Whether this would actually materialise remained to be seen, but they did a lot of preparatory work, so who knows.

This attempt to carry out some real 'therapy' I have to say, had been professionally very disappointing. It had been hyped up that so many families need help and were waiting for me – presumably to wave that ubiquitous wand. I had spent hours preparing the timetable and sessions and having Anya translate them. (Anyone want a Russian version of 'Letting Go'?) I put the lack of interest down to poor organisation and communication between Lily and this local organiser – both of whom were arch controllers. I should, in retrospect, have insisted on communicating with the local organiser myself.

After the second night in our hostel, Lily decided she and I would be better off in a hotel, and who was I, or my bowels, to argue? So Lily, Anya and I adjourned to a hotel suite. Lily took the master bedroom, I took the smaller bedroom and poor Anya took the couch – oh, and young Billy, I suspect, also enjoyed the delights of a comfortable bed.

The hotel faced the sea and so at last I got the smell of sea air. The Caspian Sea is enclosed but huge – I cannot remember figures, but large enough to be tidal. I had never seen ice formations on the edge of a sea, nor had I seen swans bobbing on the breakers!

Our evenings were spent eating, but not drinking alcohol, as it would have been insensitive to the patients we had with us. However, one evening an exception was made as we were going bowling, and at eleven p.m. we moved on to a disco – quite enjoyable, though we were all very tired by then.

The highlight of the trip had to be the banya. The grateful brother of a patient whom we were taking back to the treatment centre had arranged a private banya. It was a fabulous place, very modern – pine panelling everywhere, and very warm. There was a billiard room, a room with Jacuzzi, sauna and cold plunge pool, and a sitting room with a table groaning with fruit, snacks, beer, wine and cognac. So we ladies spent the whole evening lying around, sweating, eating, drinking and plunging into the cold water to wake us up. It was so relaxing that it was hard to tear ourselves away.

The last day was a rest day and we were taken on an excursion to a saints' place, an ancient Muslim burial ground. The first Muslim to bring Islam to Kazakhstan was apparently beheaded and his body was buried there (his head is in a museum!). The graves ranged from simple, basic ones to very elaborate mausoleums with moving inscriptions.

I later managed to track down the two Peace Corps volunteers I knew were working in Aktau. I met up with them and had my first conversation with English speakers in eight days. Their ears are probably still recovering!

The recording of our second TV programme was carried out in Russian this time, and it all went amazingly smoothly, though I found myself increasingly irritated with the smugness of one of my 'colleagues'. He appeared to have no tolerance and came across as so pious and smug it was nauseating.

After breakfast the next day I took a long walk by the sea, and when I returned for my bags and waited for the car, Billy was still ensconced in Lily's bedroom where he had gone as I left.

The farewells turned out to be a very interesting experience – *all* the hosts said something about how much they valued our visit and most of our group then responded. Gifts were exchanged and there were even tears as people hugged goodbye. A tad over the top, I felt, but as I received a Kazakh waistcoat, a conch shell and a picture of the swans on the sea at Aktau, I cannot really complain!

The journey home was pretty uneventful except that a strong icy wind blew up and covered the track in snow, so we were held up for two hours while they cleared it and the journey took fifty-three hours.

Constantly being excluded from the chitchat was beginning to seriously irritate me, and I could not decide whether I was being unrealistic in expecting Anya to interpret more. Maybe this was the reason I found myself having quite a heated argument with Lily.

She smugly confided in me of her latest plan with the pride of someone who had what she believed to be a great idea and had put it into practice and was now looking for admiration. She had not reckoned on little ole me!

To explain, she had decided that the centre and the secondary care place (Acar) should now become smoking free. Now, when I left the UK this matter was being hotly debated in most treatment centres. On the one hand, no-one can argue against the fact that to stop smoking is a good option. Timing is important, though, and to expect newly clean addicts and alcoholics to give up that prop as well is tough. In the West there are no end of support groups, counsellors, social workers, doctors and anti-smoking therapies to help those who want it, but here in Kazakhstan? Outside of the centre, there was nothing, absolutely nothing, in the way of support for recovering addicts and alcoholics and their families.

In addition, Lily's plan, in my view, was draconian: she was to initiate a directive which stated that if a patient was caught smoking then he or she would be discharged instantly. The irony was that the two patients accompanying had volunteered to start the ball rolling and set a good example. But guess who was having a sneaky fag when I stepped outside for a smoke in Aktau?

I argued the best I could for somewhat less draconian measures, and to show a little compassion and understanding for 'her' addicts. This was to no avail. Lily was convinced that if she requested this from 'her' addicts, they would comply.

Well, if discharge was the only option, sure, she was going to get overt compliance. But if my understanding of addicts' behaviour is correct, it would not be more than simply verbal compliance. She disagreed, and in the end we had to agree to disagree – of course she was the boss, so there. No sign of consulting one's staff on matters of importance, I can assure you.

So I gave up on the conversation, disgusted and furious that Lily was so sure that she had such power over 'her' addicts, and I confided in my diary, which was beginning to feel even more like my only friend.

It was also become increasingly uncomfortable to be around Billy and Lily. Their intimacy was intense, and I felt it was inappropriate, an abuse of her power and completely unethical. I was obviously not the only one who could see what was going on. Something should be said – but to whom and by whom? Lily's husband was the overall director, so what could I or anyone say without the proverbial s*** hitting the fan? She was getting away with it whilst pontificating on the evils of smoking!

Another day, Lily and I had another disagreement, this time about the tsunami of all things. I said something about how terrible it had been, and she basically said it was karma and that the people who had been affected must have done something awful in their previous lives. I was well aware of the concept of karma; it was her dismissive, judgemental attitude that riled me so much. Again we had to agree to disagree.

Thankfully we arrived in Astana, and I said my farewells (I hope the glee was not too evident!). I met up with Mike, the volunteer there who was training social workers. I was to also do a presentation, and so I would stay there for three days. I was to stay in a hotel with a room all to myself. What luxury!

Mike took me to his apartment, where he and his girlfriend made me very welcome. I suspect I talked non-stop; I was so desperate for conversation. Anya had translated less and less on the train, and I was not sorry to leave her.

Astana had been the capital now for about seven years and the government buildings were basically being built from scratch. The president's palace is like a model of the White House. For all that, it was pleasing to see so many different buildings and mostly I thought they were attractive. I especially liked the observatory from which you can see all of Astana rising out of the steppe – a bit surreal really.

The highlight of that stay had to be the Kazakh opera. The opera house was magnificent, all white and gold and sparkly with the obligatory chandeliers. The opera was written by a Kazakh composer and sung in Kazakh and all were dressed in Kazakh costumes. Not the best music I have ever heard, but very entertaining. The composer was in the audience that evening and received a standing ovation.

Then I had yet another train journey back to Pavlodar, and though it feels very strange to say so, it was quite good to be home, and boy was I looking forward to being in my own bed. Not to be! Mike and his girlfriend decided to travel with me to Pavlodar to help Tom celebrate his birthday, but as he was out when we arrived, they stayed in my bed and I slept on the floor. At least it was my floor!

We met up with Tom and eventually found a place to eat that suited us all. We were joined by one of the American volunteers and her boyfriend. Mike took an instant dislike to her and the atmosphere was very strained. After a few more vodkas at Tom's place, the tension lifted a little. We crashed out there, uncomfortably.

I had to get up in the morning for my first Russian lesson with a new teacher, Sevda. She was a lecturer at one of the universities and, as is the culture, lived with her parents despite being in her late twenties. Her room doubled as a study and bedroom, and has a green-baize-covered table with two chairs. There was a world map on the wall behind her chair and a glass-fronted cupboard full of books behind mine. She was definitely a perfectionist, and I could see these lessons were not going to be easy.

Another month was gone, and whilst it felt good that time was passing so quickly, I also wanted to slow it down. I still did not feel I was making much impact. Having said that, I did notice a subtle change in some of the things the patients said to me, the questions they asked and so on. Maybe I was having more of an influence than I realised, or maybe it was just a coincidence. Who knew, and in fact it did not really matter as long as change did occur.

Fourteen

NO SMOKING HERE

The spring festival had just taken place and the weather was somewhat spring-like for a few days, but then it snowed several times and froze over and did not feel like spring at all. I went with a teacher from one of the primary schools to watch their portrayal of spring arriving. Winter was dressed as an ageing being and was ceremoniously burned whilst a beautiful young woman was heralded in to represent the new spring. This was all done in the sunny but very cold playground, followed by the children playing a number of team games involving ski sticks, skis and sledges. All good fun.

We also celebrated Women's Day a couple of days after the UK's Mothers' Day, and I was promised that men would present me with flowers, but sadly this did not happen – mainly as I did not know many men at all! The female staff at Acar were treated to a little performance by the patients. It was marred by Lily insisting we all dance. I love dancing, but this was not a suitable occasion, and her attitude was so unctuous I wanted to curl up and die.

I later managed to pin her down for a discussion about some training I had proposed. She clearly had not read the proposal I had given her a week or so before, which annoyed me intensely; it was obviously not important enough to warrant her attention. Anyway I had some kind of permission to go ahead and organise it, though no doubt it would be sabotaged – I had no great illusions this would be any more successful than other attempts to achieve something positive.

To offset the absence of our own mothers and children for Women's Day, I invited the other volunteers, plus one or two Kazakh girls I met, and Tom as our token male, to my flat for an English tea. That was quite fun, and my guests must have enjoyed themselves as they stayed from mid-afternoon until quite late in the evening – or maybe they finally realised tea was all they were going to get! I have to say the scones turned out quite well, despite the odd flour.

The social front still left a lot to be desired, but my new Russian teacher, Sevda, and her mother took me swimming with them a couple of times. This was quite interesting, as modesty went out of the window and no-one bothered to dress or undress discretely. What is more, in the showers mothers scrubbed their daughters, daughters scrubbed their mothers, and friends scrubbed friends. I assumed it was a hangover from the village banya days.

On one occasion I was introduced to an interesting lady and she invited us back for tea. She had the only apartment I had seen which had white walls; generally the walls were covered in 1950s-type wallpaper and were not very attractive. She was interested in astrology and astronomy, and informed me that Pavlodar is on the same latitude as Stonehenge. For some reason I found this quite remarkable, and when I checked it out it did seem to be so. Now quite what that means I have no idea, but it somehow made me feel not so isolated and far from home.

The Kazakh New Year was celebrated on 21 March, which meant another day off work. This three-day event coincides with the spring equinox and was reinstated after 1988; that is, when Kazakhstan ceased to be part of the Soviet Union. It is the most celebrated of all festivals in the country. In the cities and villages yurts are erected and performances of singing and dancing take place. I wandered into the town and saw the yurts in the square and listened briefly to some singing, but I did not feel part of it at all and came home. It was a particularly bitterly cold and wet day, which did not help alleviate the slight depression I was feeling.

Neither did a lesson with Sevda. Somehow we started to talk about my younger daughter, about whom I worried constantly, when I was not worrying about myself. Our conversations often became quite deep, and after a few searching questions from Sevda, I was tearful. Drawing on her own experience (her mother is very controlling), Sevda advised me to 'back off' from my daughter and give her space to develop in her own way. Well, I would have thought I could not have backed off much more than moving halfway across the world, but psychologically of course I was still very attached.

Work took an interesting turn as Lily stuck to her edict that Acar was to be a non-smoking centre and any patient who did not stop smoking would be discharged forthwith. Several patients were discharged and others – in order to help them, you understand – were sent to the main centre in Pavlodar and locked in a room for five days. I was so appalled by this that I went to the centre to try to talk to them, only to be told that I was not allowed to talk to them, and the guard prevented me from even going near the room.

This action was so 'successful' that two of the patients who had been incarcerated subsequently returned to Acar and really could not stop smoking. They were told to leave and relapsed on heroin as soon as they hit Pavlodar. Lily's response was that it was time they left treatment and anyway it was their choice. What she failed to see was that the patients did not have choice – basically they were being blackmailed by her edict, which made them feel powerless and angry. What feelings do addicts use on? Powerlessness and anger! What grieved me more than anything was her seemingly callous attitude, which made me wonder what the motivation was. It certainly did not seem to be the patients' best interests.

Naturally it was the only topic to be talked about at Acar, and it divided the community very unpleasantly. There were those who were only too happy to 'grass up' those who were struggling and disappeared for a sneaky cigarette, in an attempt to keep 'Mama' happy and stay in her good books. Their relationship with Lily (or I should say her relationship with the patients) was, in my view, not a healthy one, but it was she who had created it.

One of the more senior volunteers asked to see me. She was clearly disturbed by these events, and spoke of her relationship with one of the other volunteers. It seemed to be very similar to sibling rivalry, and of course this was not surprising, given Lily's style of management whereby she was looked to as the 'mother'. She also told me she had reported two patients for smoking marijuana and no action had been taken. She was clearly seeing matters for what they were and it had shaken her whole belief in the centre's system. I felt very sorry for her as there was little that could be done and she had few choices if she wished to remain there.

In yet another meeting with Lily, she actually asked me to help her enforce her rule. I made some suggestions, but she did not want to hear what I had to say. She was making my position untenable. Basically she gave me the same choice she gave the patients: agree with me and do as I say, or leave!

Conversations with other 'volunteers' told me they also knew what was going on but were equally powerless.

Anya told me she was resigning at the end of March. This was something of a relief as I was not looking forward to dealing with sacking her once Lily remembered that was what she was intending. However, once she had told me, Anya then opened up to me far more than she had in the previous six months. She feared she may be anorexic, had issues with her controlling father and had learned a lot about her own situation whilst working with me. She was a sweet girl but very unworldly and sensitive. She had worked hard to learn a lot of new terms relating to my work and had started to translate many of the handouts I hoped to use on the course I was due to start soon. She had become much more adept at interpreting for me with the patients and, once they had stopped ogling her, they had accepted her position.

It was with some relief I left Pavlodar that week for Almaty and the second experience of the organisation's skill share. It was much more enjoyable than the first, as I knew more people now and also because it was in Almaty, which has a bit more life going on than either Pavlodar or indeed Semipalatinsk. The workshops were well put together, and most sessions were lively and interesting.

However, the downside was that we stayed in a sanatorium again and the food was dire! To compensate, the organisation treated us to a meal in a local Chinese restaurant and it was truly delicious. (It did not have much to beat, mind you; I had survived on cabbage, carrots and beetroot for the last four months.) Embarrassingly, I drooled over the broccoli, cauliflower, peppers and aubergine!

The two-day skill share was followed by a two-day employers' workshop which I did not enjoy. My employer, Lily, could not attend, so I could not take part in the mixed volunteer/employer exercises and I found it tedious in the extreme.

It was also marred by the fact that I had to tell the organisation's director that I had discovered a lump under my arm. As it was only about three years since I had been diagnosed with breast cancer (which had been treated successfully), it was of course taken seriously and I was despatched to consult a doctor straight away. The doctor felt, and the organisation agreed, that I should consult my consultant in the UK as soon as possible.

Janet, one of the Almaty volunteers, was great and went with me to the doctor's and generally supported me – such a change and very welcome. She invited me to dinner and, despite being ill herself and having family problems, she was lovely. We went to a yoga session that evening – yoga like I had never experienced before! The instructor had been trained in Tibet but I could not ascertain which particular school of yoga it was. He took us through various exercises for three hours, including beating us with a rolled-up mat. I remain unconvinced as to the benefits of this!

So now plans were afoot for me to return to the UK in a couple of weeks, and I was anticipating I would only be there for three weeks or so. I had such mixed feelings. I was concerned about the lump and agreed I could not ignore it, but truly felt fine and doubted it was anything significant. And it was such bad timing from the work point of view. Anya's resignation meant I had to find another interpreter and pretty damn quickly too. In addition, I had been feeling a little bit more settled and had been looking forward to seeing what delights the summer might provide. So the timing was not good, but the thought of seeing family and friends so much sooner than I had expected to was obviously very exciting.

Fifteen

BACK IN THE UK, BRIEFLY

The two or three weeks prior to my departure for the UK were a very busy time. Initially, my plan was to go to the UK, have my treatment, whatever that was, and not tell anyone I was home until I knew there was nothing to worry about. Clearly this was not going to work, so I then had some difficult phone calls to make to the family. Apart from the nature of my visit, it would be wonderful to see everybody.

After several meetings with Lily, we had detailed the courses I had proposed. We agreed I could usefully do some work with the patients who were preparing to return to their homes and wanted to help the using addicts in their hometowns. This idea of helping other users to stop or at least control their using, whilst highly commendable, is usually put on the back burner for a couple of years in the West – the newly recovering addicts build up sobriety and inner strength before trying to help others. In Kazakhstan there are few luxuries, and the idea of recovering addicts building their sobriety in a supportive environment and taking things slowly is one such. Once the patients leave treatment, there is no support whatsoever, and it seemed practical therefore to give them some training in operating a kind of buddy system and referral agency.

This then was to be my new focus. A group of twelve was handpicked – by Lily naturally! They were to receive training from me three times a week. I spent hours preparing the sessions and Anya spent hours translating the handouts and my notes for the sessions so we would both be prepared. We held a few sessions, which I think went quite well, prior to her leaving.

There was then an urgent search to find another interpreter, and I was determined to do this myself this time. I met Misha in a cafe in order to interview him away from prying eyes. He had come recommended by a fellow volunteer for whom he had done a little work previously. He was clearly keen to impress, and indeed his standard of spoken English was very good. His previous experience of interpreting was limited, but he was very charming and amusing and personable, and therefore a refreshing change from dear Anya. I decided to take him on for a probationary period, subject to references and Lily's approval, of course. In any case I had little choice, given my imminent departure for England.

We would have commenced work immediately but there was a delay due to some of Misha's papers not being available. To be fair, the amount of paperwork required for employment was extensive, to put it mildly, but it turned out Misha was not the most organised person and was not exactly diligent in producing all the requisite documents. In the meantime, I suggested he sit in on a session Anya and I were doing so he could see what was to be required of him. After the session I asked him what he thought and he proceeded to give me some feedback as to my 'performance'. Not quite what I had meant!

Misha and I managed to fit in three sessions of our training before I was due to go. We hit it off very well on a personal level and he was quick to learn new terminology. His computing skills were even worse than Anya's and this was a big drawback. However, the most important aspect of his job was to interpret what I said well, and he seemed to achieve this well. The patients liked him, though I suspected he was a tad too friendly with them, which I would have to address, given his lack of experience in a therapeutic setting where setting boundaries is essential.

Misha took me to his sister, a hairdresser, to get my hair done. It was the first time in my life that I was not asked by a hairdresser what I wanted doing. Larissa made an assessment and got to work without any further ado. I left with what I thought was a very good haircut and the promise of highlights next week.

The day came for me to depart, new hairdo and all. Misha insisted he come with me to the airport, and I was touched by his concern. I told him what time I was leaving, but he was not at my house when the taxi arrived. Sadly I started to put my bags in the boot and got into the car, and then I heard my name being screamed out. It was him, racing across the square, all hot and bothered. In he got and off we set. He told the driver to stop outside a shop and he ran inside without any explanation to me. He returned with a bottle of champagne and two plastic cups! We quickly downed a glass at the departure gate, at which I arrived just in time. Then off I went. I have no idea how Misha got back home.

My first and startling impression on being back in London was the greenness. I guess I had become used to the constant lack of colour in Pavlodar, and I found the colours almost hurt my eyes.

I was impressed with the organisation and communication between the voluntary organisation and my consultant. I was seen the day I arrived and booked in the next day to have the offending lump removed in day surgery. The only problem occurred when I was about to leave the day ward with my daughter and the wound haemorrhaged, staining my white shirt. All was sorted, and in due course I was immensely relieved to hear it indeed was nothing malignant, and I was eventually given the all-clear to return to Kazakhstan.

Then, unfortunately, there was a hitch with my visa, which held up my return by another ten days or so. The delay enabled me to see more of the children than I had anticipated and made me realise exactly what I was missing. The protracted stay gave me time to reflect, and I am not sure this was such a good thing. I found myself thinking of the stone at the water's edge: once removed, the water quickly fills the space it left. I felt sad that this was what had happened to me. The space I occupied in people's lives had all too quickly been filled by other people or things. But it was my choice to leave, and doubtless some may have interpreted that as a kind of rejection by me.

Whether it was the right decision or not, I had made my bed and I had to return to it. Interestingly I was missing my few friends and I was looking forward to the summer there and what it might have to offer. So exactly where did I feel I belonged? Part of me belonged in England with the children and grandchildren, but part of me now belonged in Pavlodar where I had a lot of unfinished business.

The initial excitement and apprehension when I first arrived had been replaced with day-to-day family matters, and I really felt it was time for me to go now. I felt I was in the way now with the family.

My visa was finally delivered, by courier, just one hour before I needed to depart for the airport. My family and I exchanged tearful farewells again, before my son drove me to the airport.

Sixteen

RETURN TO PAVLODAR

What a difference a month can make! On my return I found the weather had warmed up considerably. Consequently the heating and the hot water had been turned off, and the trees had literally burst into leaf, but unfortunately the mosquitoes had also come to life. In all the damp places the little buzzing, biting insects, some as large as birds (well, I do exaggerate slightly, but some are huge!) operated en masse. And they were relentless in their search for flesh, into which to sink their nasty little jaws, and so sneaky with it too, so that often I did not even realise they had landed until I itched.

Furthermore, it looked as if there had been torrential rain for weeks on end (though I was assured this was not the case – it was just the result of melted ice from the mountainous areas in China), and around the river which flows north to south and whose banks the city and Acar itself border there were puddles, pools and lakes – plenty of scope for the mosquitoes to reproduce and feed. So around Acar they formed clouds and they were well-nigh impossible to avoid. What is more their jaws must have been enormous as they attacked through clothing with apparent ease!

Meeting up with Tom and his new girlfriend (whom I thought was stoned) and Misha and others was lovely. And I gradually settled back into some kind of routine again.

One of my resolutions for my return was not to focus on the negatives all the time. I guess this was partly due to being reminded of some frustrations about living in the UK whilst I was there – bureaucracy I had conveniently forgotten about but which easily matched some of the red-tape procedures experienced in Kazakhstan too.

So, for example, I tried not to focus on how I waited an hour and three quarters for Misha to appear one day (he was supposedly held up waiting for my passport to be returned), which meant we missed our meeting with my revered boss, Lily. Nor would I focus on the computer that would not read a floppy disc; nor on the printer that refused to print; nor on the time spent looking for the person with the key for the office in which said computers were situated; nor on the person – any person – who might know the password for the computer; nor on the guy who pretended to be knowledgeable about computers but clearly knew sweet FA; nor on the woman who gave Misha yet another paper to translate when he was way behind with my work anyway. Finally I would desperately try to ignore the various itches all over my body from the aforementioned mosquitoes!

I would focus on the fact that I went to the post office on my own, bought a stamp, had my PO box opened and found post in there which had been addressed to the centre but which some clued-up person had put in my box for me. I would also focus on visiting the visa office, again by myself, and managing to retrieve my passport, duly stamped and registered, without any hitches.

The same day, I found some cheap compost for my pots in which I hoped to grow some flowers. This was no mean feat, as the bags I had found were, I thought, very overpriced. This particular shopkeeper went to a stall down the road and came back with a small bag, about a quarter of the price of her bags, and the soil, I think I understood her to say, was from the *dachas* – well, if it was good enough for them to grow their veggies, then it was good enough for my nicotiana, I reckoned. Time would surely tell!

To top it all, I bought two bunches of lilies of the valley from a little old lady on the street for a whole forty pence, and in addition, came home and made myself a tasty meal for once. Don't know why it was, but my culinary skills in Kazakhstan would have rendered Jamie completely speechless, but that night was an exception.

Actually I ate rather well the night before too, but not through my own endeavours. Sevda invited me to a meal for her twenty-eighth birthday, and her mum had prepared a feast. The tradition was to keep producing food until you practically rolled from the table, groaning. She produced pumpkin and pineapple salad, new potatoes and mushrooms, mixed salad, chicken salad, cooked chicken and roast potatoes. Cherries, apricots, chocolate nuts, chocolates, chocolate cake, wine, martini and tea finished it off!

There were just four guests, one of whom was Sevda's oldest friend from school. She scarcely said a word, and left the table to read a book. She apparently had a car – a rare phenomenon – but declined to give the rest of us a lift home.

Sevda's father turned up later; he also hardly spoke, and went out, then came home and disappeared to his room. I noticed that Sevda's mother, despite being a doctor and, I assumed, well educated, fussed over her husband the whole time, even giving him some money when he went out.

Of the other two guests, one spoke very good English and she tried to interpret occasionally. Otherwise I was left to guess as to their conversation or drift into my own thoughts. Sadly Russian anecdotes and jokes lose much in the translation! Thankfully I had the photos from my recent trip in my bag and they proved to be a good way of communicating.

Sevda was off to Germany next week, so we would have no lessons for another three weeks.

Work, unfortunately, proved to be quite predictable in that over half of the 'students' who started my course had left in the time I was away. Some left as they had had enough of the restrictions at Acar, and quite honestly who could blame them? Others left either because they drank or smoked. So I recruited a few more raw recruits, but I didn't have too much hope they would stay the course either.

One night I arranged to meet Misha to go to the theatre. He was late and I felt very conspicuous waiting as a busload of patients turned up from Acar. He rolled up eventually with some cock-and-bull story, but we had a lovely evening, finishing at my flat with a few beers.

Then he said he had something to tell me, and my heart sank. I knew it was going to be bad news, but I was not prepared for the reality. Whilst I was away he had been stopped by the police whilst getting a lift from a friend. They were both charged with possession of an illegal substance: namely heroin. This was seriously bad news. The punishment for such a crime in Kazakhstan is severe, possibly three years, and conditions in the prisons are dreadful. In addition, the fact he was working at a treatment centre really was not to be desired, if in fact he was an addict himself.

I should have fired him on the spot. But then I did not hire him, Lily did, and I figured what she did not know would not hurt her. This is a decision I am not proud of, but I needed an interpreter. Life was difficult enough anyway, with me struggling to keep the courses going, and I wanted to believe that he was not aware of the presence of this substance in the car when he got in. In all honesty, I chose to believe him because I liked him. I enjoyed working with him, he did a good job and we had a few laughs, interesting discussions and debates. Quite frankly I did not want to lose this, and so I decided not to inform on him but to help him get some justice.

In any case, we had to put all this to one side as we had a meeting with Lily later that day in, of all places, a prison! There was talk of initiating some programme in-house for the addicts there.

A couple of days later Misha's lawyer requested a deferment in order to give him time to raise some money. Misha told me his only hope to avoid a custodial sentence was to bribe his lawyer and, through her, the judge. This bribery, I understood, was standard practice. So Misha was unable to work for days whilst he tried to raise enough money for said bribe. The paltry sum he did raise produced a wry laugh from his lawyer – in retrospect I suspect she was as bent as five-bob note and put the wind up him to ensure her own cut.

The whole affair raised so many issues and problems, both for Misha and for me. I really should have reported the matter to the organisation, and then Lily would probably have suspended him temporarily, until the outcome of the court case at least. But if Misha were to lose his job, what chance would he have of paying off any money he had borrowed for the bribe? And what would I do in the meantime? I may as well have packed up and gone, and I really did not want to. If we could limp along for the time being then so be it. We would deal with the outcome as and when we needed to.

However, I had to decide whether Misha was a suitable person to act as interpreter in a treatment centre. If I really believed this was a one-off mistake, I would plead for his innocence, but the fact I was questioning it at all spoke volumes.

Musing on this, on my way to aerobics, I decided after all, I would have to sack Misha and report the whole matter to Lily and the voluntary organisation. I came home, showered, cooked and then felt so sad at the whole situation. Misha called me and was witty and funny and so 'sparky' – how could he be with all this hanging over his head? I was laughing and crying with him, and I said if he went down then I would leave Kazakhstan, as that would be the final straw.

If I am truly honest, my feelings for him were definitely clouding my judgement. I was caught in the trap that so many family members of addicts are caught in. When they are not with you, you can make total sense, you see them for what they are and you know you should practise 'tough love' and not enable the using behaviour to continue. Then they turn up and they are funny and charming and loving, and your heart takes over and your resolve weakens.

Lily's behaviour was becoming more and more outrageous too. Her relationship with her lap dog was obvious for all to see, a 'senior' patient had been discharged for seeing something he should not have, and the gossipmongers said she was claiming benefits for fictitious patients. She clearly did not want to discuss the prison project with me, and why, in the name of Allah, was she talking about sporting activities? Was it just possible that she was losing the plot altogether?

Then it became apparent that the current political scene may override any concerns I had as to my possible effectiveness or what to do about Misha. It seemed some of the MPs had become somewhat paranoid as to the presence of foreigners in Kazakhstan (one assumes some recent events in the other 'stans', Ukraine etc., had a knock-on effect). Their plan was to pass a new law as soon as they possibly could to prevent foreigners from heading up any non-governmental organisations and to prevent any non-governmental organisation being funded by any means other than within Kazakhstan. In addition they wanted to tax all grants donated to any such organisations.

In effect this would close down many of the organisations aided by our voluntary organisation. If indeed this law was passed, we would have to pull out of Kazakhstan forthwith –well, in reality this would probably take at least three months. Quite how quickly this would come into effect was unknown, but the buzz was that they wanted to pass the law before the parliamentary recess next month. The fact that I 'worked' for a governmental organisation was irrelevant, I guess, though the timing would probably coincide with my end of placement in any case.

Seventeen

THE QUEEN'S BIRTHDAY

Today Misha was to go and see his lawyer and then come to my flat for brunch to report back. Hence work was not an option, so I busied myself cleaning, trying to learn some Russian verbs, reading and sunbathing – on the kitchen floor! The balcony was very small and the sun came streaming through the door, so I lay a blanket on the floor and wallowed in the delicious heat for an hour or two.

The day wore on and by four p.m. Misha still had not met his lawyer. So just what had he been doing?

The next weekend Mike arrived with an old friend and we met up with others, visiting the orthodox church and wandering down by the river, drinking and chatting. We spent a lovely weekend together, and so I felt sad to wave them off on the Sunday evening. A phone call from my sister and mum helped to shake me out of my self-pity, though my sister's loss of voice was worrying.

Back to work, I reckoned I fed about thirty-two mosquitoes in a day. They were unbelievable!

We had a session with a mother of an addict and I found myself wondering how it was affecting Misha. I could not shake the suspicion that he was an addict himself, though most of the time he held it together. That day he was wearing a short-sleeved shirt and I swear I saw track marks on his arm. Then Mr Denial broke in and I decided I must have been mistaken. I did ask him about his arm and he told some story, which I knew was untrue.

He then said with a smile, 'Do you think I should go into treatment?'

I replied, 'It doesn't matter what I think, but if you feel you should then do so.'

I had no idea how serious the question was, but the very fact he raised it, even in fun, suggested he knew he had a problem.

He was gradually getting the money together (not from me, I might add – he already owed me quite a lot and there was precious little chance of getting it back), so that he may gradually sort out his mess. But I still had my 'mess' to attend to. I had to devise a strategy.

The next day was court day. We spent the evening with a bottle of cognac and got somewhat drunk as we prepared for the worst-case scenario. What else could we do when there was a lurking fear that this may be our last evening together and his last of freedom? He had implored me to tell nobody and he had told no-one, not even his family.

We talked about how I was to collect his bag and pay from Acar, and how I would get cigarettes, tea and sweets in for him. His tone remained fairly jolly, but goodness knows what he was really feeling. I so wanted to offer some physical comfort, but I managed to cling on to some self-control and send him home at not too late an hour so he could be bright eyed and bushy tailed for the morrow.

The next morning, I tried to call him at the friend's house where he was staying, to no avail. I made my way to the courthouse well before nine a.m., nodded to his lawyer and waited outside for Misha to appear. The minutes ticked by and there was no sign of him. I experienced a whole range of emotions as I waited – anger that he was late, fear that he may have done something stupid, and frustration that I could not get in touch with him as he had no mobile phone. Finally I put on an appeasing act for his lawyer, imploring her not to give up on him. The judge had appeared by now and I really thought this would be the end for Misha, whatever had happened.

Twenty-nine minutes later he strode into view, sweating profusely, unwashed, unshaven and stinking of stale alcohol. Not the best way to impress a judge. Where he had been was not important; I was just worried as to what would happen now.

To my amazement the judge agreed to hear his case. This country was full of surprises. We entered the court room, and I expected it to be full so I could be pretty inconspicuous. Not so! There were just six of us (judge, prosecutor, defence lawyer, secretary, Misha and me). The hearing followed the usual procedures, but it then transpired that the judge was curious as to my involvement. I realised I had perhaps been unwise in attending.

Anyway, having heard all the evidence for and against, the judge postponed his judgement (I suspected so he could check on my credentials) until the next day. We left and made our way home.

The next day was phenomenally long. I had made the wise decision not to attend court again, but made Misha promise to ring as soon as he had some news. The later it got, the more I was convinced I would never see or hear from him again. As the day wore on I decided finally to blow the whistle. I went into the centre and told Lily the bare bones of the story.

Misha finally rang late that night. The penalty would be a fine plus two years' probation. What a relief, expressed in the time-honoured shedding of tears, followed by silence from him. The lack of contact drove me crazy and there were few other friends around with whom I could distract myself or in whom I could confide.

Two days later, Misha rolled up with his friend JB, plus a bottle of wine, cognac, salad and crisps! We tried to reconnect, but I had a feeling he was regretting having told me the whole story and he had become somewhat reticent. I wanted to know, for example, when he had to meet his probation officer, so we could plan our work accordingly, but he avoided any mention of the whole affair. He was also feeling unwell – I think just a cold, for which the remedy was to stick a cotton wool bud doused in diesel up one's nose!

A few days later, Misha had a birthday. To his embarrassment, I bought him a present. We went on a river trip and had a lovely evening.

The next Friday, we arrived on the early-morning bus at Acar to prepare for the training in the afternoon, only to be told all but three patients were going to be out that day and therefore they would not be able to attend the course. Next, I was asked why I had not gone to Bayanaul with everyone else. It seemed the rest of the staff had gone on an outing to our local beauty spot, which I had not seen yet, and no-one had thought to tell me! Biting back my disappointment, hurt and fury, I went to prepare some handouts for the next session, only to find none of the computers were working and my precious flip chart had disappeared!

That was the final straw for me. I desperately needed to get out of there. No way was I going to wait for the bus. My frustration and hurt had reached hitherto unknown depths. The problem was how to escape when the nearest local bus stop was about five kilometres away and it was very hot and the mosquitoes, midges and horse flies were relentless. Being resourceful, I asked Misha to ask that the pony and trap be prepared. The horse was not shod, so he could only go cross-country to the main road. This suited me fine, and we were taken over rough ground to the main road, whereupon we had no option but to hitch – a phenomenon not that common in Kazakhstan, but where there is a will there is a way!

I felt well protected by my interpreter (when we had been discussing his duties, at the start of his working with me, we had joked about him being my protector, so I called on this duty that day). Our moods were good and we found ourselves giggling at the silliest things – like the superstition about whistling: if you whistle, you will never have any money, and so that is why Misha never had any.

One guy finally took pity on us, or maybe he possessed the quality, unusual in Kazakhstan, of acting out of curiosity! I felt this to be a minor, if pathetic, triumph. We eventually arrived home and spent the rest of the day on my balcony, chatting and generally enjoying each other's company.

This, however, was a little blip in an otherwise quite depressing state. Being left out of the staff trip had affected me enormously, on top of all the other problems I had. I found myself either in tears or on the verge of tears much of the time, and waking very early in the mornings. I would worry about the various problems and then something would happen to buck me up and I would feel better – at least on the surface.

I spent a great evening with various volunteers and I spent the next day with Mike and a friend of his who was over for a short holiday. That evening we went to a party for a colleague of Tom's. As usual there was so much food to be consumed between the numerous vodka toasts.

A very pleasant twenty-four hours in Astana followed. We volunteers were invited to the Embassy's celebration of the Queen's birthday the day before. This was not the sort of event I would normally attend, but thanks to that pretty miserable day when I was excluded from the staff outing, I decided I was in need of a change of scene. So a Filipino volunteer, Misha and I took the overnight train to Almaty. We were met by one of the

Astana volunteers, Elizabeth, in Astana, and we went to her flat to shower and breakfast.

Then we spent a few hours sightseeing – I had seen much of the city before, but it was worth a second look. We went first to the new mosque – a stunningly beautiful building, white with gold domes outside and all blues and white inside. I found it very calming. From there we went to the area where all the new building was going on for the capital, including the observatory. The president's palace, government buildings, ministries and embassies would all be built in this area north of the river, extending into the never-ending steppe.

Rumour had it that some of this new building was not started on very sound foundations – literally, as well as metaphorically. The money for the construction came from the oil-drilling rights, which were sold off to several different countries. Many people were not happy that the money had not been spent on improving the infrastructure generally, rather than on these obvious displays of opulence to be enjoyed by very few.

We made our way back to Elizabeth's to shower and make ourselves pretty for the ambassador. The cocktail party was held in a superb five-star hotel, and once we had been 'received' by the ambassador and his wife, we simply ate and drank ourselves to a standstill – poor, impoverished volunteers that we were! The tables were stacked with good food, including little goujons of fish and French fries wrapped in the *Financial Times*. Thankfully there were just two short toasts, from the ambassador and the deputy minister for foreign affairs.

I was not sure who all the other guests were, but certainly there were representatives from other embassies, all furiously working out who had sent the top man and the deputy. I met one lady who had been in Kazakhstan for two years with her husband, who worked for one of the oil companies. Interestingly her impressions, despite having a very different lifestyle to mine, were not dissimilar: she thought that corruption, nepotism, distrust of foreigners and being overly bureaucratised was preventing this country from developing further. In addition, the current president had been in power since the split from the USSR, and whilst most people I spoke to said he had done a good enough job, it really was time for fresh ideas. The problem was there was no one who could be trusted to take over. After most people had left, I had an interesting and surprisingly frank chat with a high-ranking diplomat whose impressions were also similar. I found it quite heartening – to have my ideas and opinions validated in this way helped to lift my self-esteem at least a little.

The temperature that day, by the way, was about thirty-four degrees, and so another shower, change and rest was required before we set off again – this time for the river and park. Misha had waited at Elizabeth's for us while we went to the reception but he now joined us.

Astana is much more pleasing to the eye architecturally than Pavlodar, but it had nowhere near so many trees and of course it was more bustling than dear old Pavlodar. I cannot believe I just wrote that, but I have to confess, that is how I felt!

So back to the park which, as far as I could see, had not a single flower but in little clearings there were fairground rides. Attempting to adopt a holiday mood, Misha and I went on the Big Dipper. This was not without some fear and trepidation, especially when the operator was saying things like 'We've had no accidents yet' and 'Don't worry, we have no insurance'. So the somewhat mildness and brevity of the ride was offset by the fear of 'Will I get off this in one piece?'. Well, we did, having enjoyed the adrenalin rush.

We finished our day off at a cafe and boarded the night train back to Pavlodar with no sign of any drunks in the proximity. You may imagine my horror when, on waking at three that morning (my birthday, to boot) on the train, I found my face swelling to very abnormal proportions again. I just wanted to put a bag over my head before burying myself in the sand somewhere. When we arrived at Pavlodar, therefore, I made a quick exit for the tram and went home. I had no idea what had caused it this time, but it certainly was not an allergy to the cold. I could not face talking to a doctor who probably had no clue either but rather than admit it would make all kinds of ridiculous suggestions. So I would just skulk at home and hope it went of its own accord.

In the political arena the NGO law was passed initially by the lower house but had to pass in the upper house too, and they were likely to raise objections as the foreign community was gradually making their feelings known. So it was still a matter of 'wait and see', but any crazy ideas I may have fleetingly had about extending my contract had evaporated, and I knew I would definitely leave in September, so the law would not affect me personally. (Thereby began another little saga, in that the precious visa for which I had waited three weeks in the UK would expire on 9 September – two days short.)

An email from my son lifted my spirits: he and his girlfriend had just got engaged. It was so nice to get some good news amidst all this angst.

Receiving cards from family and friends also cheered me a little, and the day after my birthday some friends came round to party. Misha and his sister gave me a beautiful illustrated book on Kazakhstan which would be much treasured.

Eighteen

MISHA'S PROBLEMS INCREASE

Over the following couple of weeks, I experienced a roller-coaster of emotions. A pattern began to emerge with dear Misha which was hard to cope with. He had moments of confiding in me and apparently opening his heart, followed by being distant, both literally and emotionally. During one of his confidences he told me about his over-controlling and over-protective mother – no surprise there, as all mothers in Kazakhstan appeared to have this 'quality'! His father was constantly grumpy, stubborn and, I suspected, an alcoholic. Misha was often expected to babysit his niece, often without warning and despite work commitments. Certainly some of his excuses for his lateness were because of this, but I could now rarely distinguish between his truths and falsehoods.

His lateness either for work or for pleasure was beginning to be beyond a joke. For example, he missed a concert, turning up as it ended. On a work day we arranged to work on a handout, and he turned up an hour and a half late, worked for a while and then disappeared again, not telling me where he was going. The problem, of course, was that we were mixing business with pleasure, and whilst I had no right to question his movements outside of work, during work hours I certainly did. The boundaries had become too foggy.

He was late again for a session, so I started without him. He was late for our meeting with Lily – but then she was too. Then he turned on the charm and humour, pleading with me not to be angry today. And everything was hunky dory again... wasn't it?

So there I was nearly at the end of ten months, and I was totally undecided what to do in mid-September when my year was up. The two courses I started were going quite well in that they seem to be well received. One of the psychologists (so called) who organised for her students to attend my course wondered why I did not stay longer as she had more students who could benefit from the course. Naturally I was tempted, as it was good to finally feel I had something to offer which may actually be gratefully received.

Lily said she would like me to stay, but I could not for the life of me work out why, other than for her to boast about their Western 'specialist'. I needed to have a proper meeting with her to discuss objectives and such like matters, but had not succeeded in doing this yet. In addition, I had heard that one of the NGOs was looking for a volunteer to work with their families. I needed to make enquiries.

The long-awaited plan for me to set up a parents' support group got off to a very bad start. I was told, the evening before, to be there for half past eleven. So I duly arrive at eleven, only to find that the parents were told ten thirty, and guess what – they gave up and left! If you want lessons in how to set yourself up for failure, look no further than Kazakhstan. Would I never learn to take control of things that are important to me? However, one mother had waited, so we spent over an hour with her and all was not completely wasted.

There was so much to chew over, and all of this in the light of not knowing the future of voluntary organisations in Kazakhstan. Our director had been on leave and so no decision would be made until his return, and opinion was truly divided as to the impact the new law would actually have. The NGOs seem to be rallying (in my opinion, far too late) and trying to put pressure on the president to radically amend the law. So, we could be out by December, and even if I did extend my contract, it could only be for three months. I thought sometimes that might be bearable; it would give me some thinking time.

Socially, life was a little more acceptable. There were a couple more American volunteers in town, so I had a merry band of seven volunteers with whom to chat, plus one or two locals I was gradually getting to know. This was just as well, as during the last two to three months I had seen little of Tom. He had been smitten with one of the local girls. Sadly for him, she turned out to be a control freak and put pressure on him to have his hair cut, buy new shoes, clean up his apartment and so on. Now Tom is a very laidback sort of guy and this did not go down too well with him. In addition, tradition dictated that the guy (even an impoverished volunteer) pay for everything, and so two months down the line he almost passed out when he saw his bank statement. Eventually he decided enough was enough, as she either could not or would not understand why he was not happy any more. So he tried to finish with her, but of course she would not let go that easily.

We all went to a huge open-air concert. There was a great build-up for this band from the West (which none of us had heard of). It was a beautiful evening and for once the mosquitoes were not too busy, but what a big disappointment when the band finally came on – they were truly awful. The locals seemed to appreciate them, but everything is relative, I guess.

We left and went to the strangest cafe I had seen so far (and I had seen some weird ones, believe me). This had two main rooms, one of which was completely panelled in pine and the other panelled in birch, but the split trunks were laid end on –very odd.

The next day ten of us had planned a long-awaited picnic. We were to meet at my flat, and then walk down to the ferry which would take us to the other side of the river where, we were assured, the water would not be quite so polluted. Gradually we started to assemble until we were only waiting for Tom (and of course Misha, but I was not holding my breath on that one). Then Tom, plus one of the American volunteers, arrived with two Kazakh guys in tow, one of whom was very drunk – well, it was one p.m.! They had met in a shop and decided they were going to accompany us on our picnic. The drunk guy could not string a sentence together but was able to make a grab at one of the young females. Despite her clearly not welcoming his advances, he persisted until she kicked him off the chair. We persuaded his mate to take him away, which he eventually did, but this all took time.

The rest of the day passed in a very relaxed fashion – we chatted and ate, and I swam in the very murky waters to cool off (but afterwards I obsessed about having a shower at the very earliest opportunity). Misha of course did not appear, and I tried not to feel hurt.

That night I slept badly. This was becoming a regular occurrence. The barking dogs, the oppressive heat, the mosquitoes, the occasional noisy drunk, plus the constantly churning thoughts going round my head all conspired to keep sleep at a distance.

The following day, after work, food and a few drinks, Misha told me he had something to ask me. My heart sank.

'Katochka, what would you say if I told you I was HIV positive?'

There was a long pause whilst I thought of an appropriate response.

'Oh, Misha, I would say that is very sad, very sad indeed. But I would want to help you in any way I could.'

My heart was beating so hard I could hardly hear myself speak. I struggled to keep my emotions under control. By now I was kneeling on the floor near his chair. I turned and did the only thing I could do: I hugged him. We both cried.

Gradually we started talking again, and he told me he had already checked in at the AIDS clinic, but there was little that could be done. Retroviral drugs were not easily available, so the prognosis long term was not good. I started to fuss, but clearly he did not want this. So we eventually parted, fondly and sadly. I found myself wondering whether this was the cause of his constantly blowing hot and cold and not allowing himself to sustain a closeness.

This news changed nothing, and I continued to feel lonely and sad when Misha was not with me, and elated when he was. I tried my best to distract myself with other friends and go to the disco, hang out with Tom and meet up with Misha's friend JB. One evening I went out with my Russian teacher and another of her friends. We went down to the riverside where they wanted to sing karaoke. There were a number of stalls where you could sing at the top of your voice – in or out of tune, it mattered not. As we were later going to a club, I had a lot of bare skin exposed, which, down by the river, the mosquitoes fully enjoyed, and I was bitten all over. But overall it was fun.

One Sunday Misha took me to his family's *dacha*. It must have been one of the furthest from the city; it took a good forty-five minutes to get there on the bus. Most families live in the apartments, such as I described before, but many also have a glorified allotment called a *dacha* where they grow the families' vegetables and fruit. They also have a hut or small bungalow where they keep the tools and store the vegetables, and they can stay there overnight. Since these *dachas* are outside the city, it is blissfully peaceful and quiet there, and I instantly felt chilled.

We spent hours gathering raspberries, redcurrants and white currants, and then drinking beer and tea and eating the fruit. Very pleasant, and I so appreciated the quiet. I had not realised just how noisy it was in the city. I suddenly realised, there at the *dacha*, with the one person who had come to mean so much to me, that I felt the happiest I had been in all my time in Kazakhstan.

But the roller-coaster was relentless. After another pleasant evening spent with Misha, I was pretty sure money was missing from my purse. I so wanted to deny he could be the culprit and I thought of all the other possibilities – none of which stood up. Would he really steal from me? When I told him I was missing some money, he appeared completely unconcerned, but then what did I expect? I did not hear from him for a few days after that.

The next Saturday, we were to hold another parents' support meeting. Having checked and rechecked the start time, nevertheless Misha was late again. As luck would have it, there was a visiting Russian psychologist who had asked to join in the session. She spoke good English, so we decided to go ahead without Misha. Sometime later, whilst one mother was tearfully telling her story, Misha barged in, so I waved him away, somewhat angrily. He was waiting when we finished and was clearly upset at my dismissing him, so he stomped off in high dudgeon.

He returned sometime later as high as a kite. This I could no longer ignore, despite any warm feelings I might harbour for him. I decided that first thing Monday morning I would give him a formal verbal warning.

Fate had other ideas! That evening, as I prepared for a night in, Tom called me, out of the blue, to say he and some friends were going to the jazz cafe which was opening that night, and to get there a.s.a.p.! I went as I was, grabbing my bag without taking out unnecessary items. It was a great night. Live jazz was new to Pavlodar and there was a great atmosphere. The previous administration had a saying: 'Listen to jazz today, betray the motherland tomorrow'. Kazakhs were starting to really appreciate having the freedom to let their hair down.

We left the jazz cafe as a group, and when we reached the main road they all went left and I headed right for my flat. I was immediately aware I was being followed by two guys. I stopped on a pretext of tying my laces and they passed, but I saw them wait in the shadows of my building.

For once there was not a soul around, and so they took their chance. One grabbed me round my neck, while the other pulled my bag off my shoulder. I lost control of my bladder, but unlike stories I have read of others in similar situations, I did not find it difficult to find my voice, and I screamed and yelled abuse at them. But they ran off and either no-one heard or no-one wanted to hear.

In my bag was my purse, credit cards, house keys, passport, mobile phone, diary, address book and so on. (This was not what I would normally carry around, but having left the flat in a hurry, I had just grabbed my bag.) So what do you do at one in the morning with no keys, no money and no phone? The little local kiosk was not open, so I called on a friend who lived nearby, but she either she did not hear my knocking or she was too scared to open her door, as was my neighbour. I was, by now, in a sorry state. The reality was beginning to hit me and I was feeling very frightened, uncomfortable and sorry for myself.

There was nothing for it but to flag down a taxi and explain in my 'exquisite' Russian that I had been mugged, had no money and needed to find a phone. It was a risk but I had little to lose. He turned out to be a good guy, and took me to another friend's apartment, but he did not hear the doorbell. Finally we went to the police station, where I used the phone to call Misha and the taxi driver helped me to explain to the police what had happened.

Misha arrived and they started to take my statement. I found it difficult to give descriptions, as the two guys were wearing hoods and it was dark.

After what seems like endless questions, one of the policemen said, 'I think this may help!' He opened a drawer and took out a bottle of vodka and some glasses. 'It has been a long night for us too,' he added. I was not convinced the vodka would aid my memory, but it did help me to relax me a little.

We eventually staggered back to Misha's house, where I was given his mother's bed. I did not enquire where she would sleep in this two-roomed apartment!

In the morning I was force-fed blinis – small pancakes – and then I arranged for my landlady to meet me at the flat to let me in. We got a spare key cut, and changed one of the three locks, so at least I was home and safe again. Replacement passports could take six weeks, so heaven knew when I should be allowed to leave this 'country that common sense forgot'.

Later that day, I got a call from a guy who said he had found my bag. Apparently this was not so unusual, as a 'reward' was better than trying to flog the contents of my bag. So in line with the advice from the police, I arranged to meet him with three detectives in the close vicinity. We waited for forty-five minutes, and even by Kazakh time he should have turned up by then, so we went home.

A hugely swollen lip was the result of all this, reinforcing for me that the swellings I had been experiencing were not so much an allergy as stress related. I consulted another doctor, who prescribed some medication.

I arranged a meeting with an NGO to discuss the possibility of my working there after September. Yes, I was, despite everything, still considering staying on! The draw was that they were definitely signed up to work with families, which I desperately wanted to do. They even had a definite plan which could be workable.

Two days later, the telephone rang at half one in the morning. It was Misha, sounding very distressed. He had been accused of stealing the mobile phone of one of our students.

This story goes like this: after our session that day, one of my students had realised her mobile was missing, and for some reason decided Misha was the culprit. As we had all been leaving the centre, she had arranged for everyone to be searched, but strangely neither Misha nor I were searched and we left, completely unaware of the situation. That evening she took her burly boyfriend, plus three others for good measure, to Misha's apartment, where they confronted him. She said she had evidence, but declined to declare it. He denied doing any such thing, and once the shouting match was over, they eventually left.

The next day, Misha was picked up and detained for five hours by the police, as this girl and her father, who was some local dignitary, had accused him of theft. There was no paperwork, he was not read his rights, they did not ask for his statement, and the police officer, the girl and her bully of a father badgered and physically assaulted him until he finally agreed to sign a paper which stated that he would pay them the equivalent of hundred pounds within two days. Apparently he crossed out the bit which said 'for the mobile phone I stole'.

Well, since I had been mugged, I had no money and no cards with which to access cash, so I was unable to help, and in any case would rather not be a part of this blackmail. I spent a long time trying to persuade Misha to consult a lawyer or the director of the centre – anyone – but he was convinced he had no choice.

We went to the centre to watch the CCTV footage which showed everybody toing and froing from the room where we held the course. It was clear that at no time was Misha alone in the room, thus exonerating him. But even this did little to change his mind. Eventually I talked to a psychologist who was visiting from Siberia and who was present that day, and she agreed to assist.

Misha agreed to talk to a friend who was a prosecutor, and they went to meet this bully father and told him that if he had a case to present, he must do so legally. So that told him, huh? Not a chance!

Three days later Misha was picked up by six guys and driven around the city while they demanded this hundred pounds. He was allowed to make one call on their mobile, so he called me, forgetting I had neither cash nor cards with which to acquire cash. He was beaten and dumped on the basis he would produce cash or the phone by four p.m. the next day.

Both he and his friends told me there was absolutely no choice. The police would be useless, and even if they were not and did arrest these guys, they would have friends who would make sure Misha was punished for grassing them up. He described this setup as being like the mafia, and indeed it did seem to be so.

That day was spent driving around in a friend's van, trying to raise the cash. The money was eventually raised, though how on earth it would be repaid I had absolutely no idea. The specific phone was purchased, but when they went to the appointed meeting place, no one turned up. So they went round to the girl's house to hand it over.

This demonstrated again corruption, intrigue and abuse of power in a developing country. It made me feel very uncomfortable. Given Misha's history, I could not help but wonder what truth there might have been in it all – though he certainly had nothing to show for it. I suspected there was much more to it all than I would ever know.

For what it is worth, my hunch was that this girl, spoiled rotten by her doting but bully of a father, was terrified of him and dared not tell him she had lost her precious phone, so she chose Misha as her scapegoat. If not that, then something even more sinister was afoot.

Nineteen

THE WEDDING

In the middle of all this distress I went to the wedding of one of the other volunteers' interpreters. It was to be held in Bayanaul, a resort near the bride's village, and it just happened to be about the only beautiful spot in this part of the country. It was to be a very beautiful traditional Kazakh wedding, but my heart was heavy, worrying about Misha and feeling unbelievably angry at the injustice of it all.

The bus ride there was uneventful and we were met and taken to the resort. The scenery was beautiful, but the resort itself was scruffy and dirty and there was a long debate as to where we should pitch our tents. We choose a kind of courtyard, which turned out to be the entrance to the zoo park! Now forget Chessington and think Pets Corner at Longleat. The toilets were stinking, but we washed and changed as best we could.

The ceremony was to take place on the terrace of one of the cafes around the resort, and the bride managed to surpass all previous experiences by being a whole hour late, by which time we were starving and dying for a drink! The Kazakh bride was beautiful, in a long pale-gold dress, and the German groom was his usual handsome self – a stunning pair. The ceremony was very brief but quite touching, and bizarrely ended with a *baboushka* hurling sweets at everyone!

The meal was an endless succession of speeches and toasts, and food was discreetly eaten between each. The MC was loud and so distorted as to be incomprehensible (not that we volunteers could have understood in any case), and there was the occasional song from random folk who thankfully broke up the tedious speeches.

At last – some three or four hours later; I don't recall and wish now I had drunk a lot more than I did – we adjourned to the terrace to dance the night away, but mostly people drifted away after the first few dances. Our second campsite turned out to be next to the open-air nightclub and within easy hearing distance of all the other cafes in the area. So not much sleep that night – and I was cold.

One of the other volunteers, a black Peace Corps volunteer, received endless attention. Of course, despite Kazakhstan being multi-ethnic, there were none other than white or off-white, so she stood out, which piqued amusement and curiosity. She must have had her picture taken at least twenty times in those few days. Personally I found it disrespectful, but I do not think they meant to be, and she was so quiet and shy she would not refuse.

We spent another three days there and it was lovely, though not without stress. Where would we pitch our tents tonight? Why not the Scout site? So we did, not that there was a Scout in sight at that point, just semi-drunken people around. Toilets – I will skip over that; I have absolutely no wish to recall them. Wash basins and showers were passable.

The lake and mountains were truly beautiful, and we climbed and swam and rowed and pedaloed and sunbathed (when it was not raining) our way through those three days. On the Sunday, in pouring rain, we went to find some botanical gardens. As we wandered around – in the pouring rain - it occurred to me what a mixed nationality group we were - (British, Kazakh, Russian, Filipino, German, French/German, American), and of course the common language was English. The gardens turned out to be little more than a trail through a wood, so we about-tailed and headed back. We made for one of the yurts and filled up on tea and cake – delicious.

That evening we went to a disco, but our enjoyment was marred by a couple of fights and the usual unwelcome attention for our black friend. We retired to bed in the early hours. Somehow we ended up with three of us in our two-man tent. I woke up squashed and cold and dying to empty my bladder. Nothing for it but to use the stinking cesspit.

We returned on a bus crammed with people, which made for a very stuffy and uncomfortable three hours, but we had no choice (there is absolutely no point getting uptight about things you cannot change in any case, and I was getting better with that).

Back in Pavlodar I was advised to put an advert on the local television, asking for any information regarding my stolen bag and possessions. Three people responded to my ad, saying they had my passport. Strange, I thought I only had one! I waited on a call from the detective who was supposed to be dealing with my case, though heaven alone knew when that would be.

Irtysh river, Pavlodar in summer

The lake at Bayanaul

Twenty

ANOTHER FALL

A meeting with Lily was a tad more productive than usual and she actually expressed some sympathy about the loss of my bag! Well, better late than never, I guess.

Now I had both Misha and his friend JB to assist me. The episode with the student and her mobile phone had, understandably, depressed Misha. I tried to persuade him to brave it out, but to no avail: he was determined to end his contract. JB, an excellent English speaker, was the obvious replacement for the remaining time I had.

We left JB working on the final handout for my course and I brought Misha home to try to arrange a visit to see the woman who said she definitely had my passport. The detective told us we should not go alone. He visited her, and apparently was met with a volley of abuse; she refused to speak to anyone other than myself.

So Misha and I set off to this woman's flat one Friday evening. With some trepidation, and not a whole lot of confidence, we knocked on the door. An extremely large lady opened it and enveloped me in a huge hug! She was very exuberant and obviously extremely pleased to see me. She invited us into the kitchen, where she was entertaining three equally large friends. The kitchen was overflowing with food (mostly meaty things) and there was a three-quarters-empty two-litre bottle of vodka on the side. No wonder they were all very jolly. She insisted we sit down to have a few drinks, listen to their singing, chat and have a jolly good time!

No mention was made of my passport, and I began to think it was all some kind of horrid joke. It never seemed to be quite the time to ask, and

I realised I was becoming very drunk. At last there was a slight pause in the conversation and singing, and I asked her about the passport. Off she went and she came back and produced with a great flourish not only my passport but also my address book.

I was truly delighted. I thanked her profusely and offered her some reward, which she steadfastly refused. I went to stand to make our farewells only to find my legs would hardly support me. Misha had to half-carry me home, much to my embarrassment. Fortunately it was not too far. He very carefully put me to bed and then took his leave sadly – but I was too inebriated to do anything else.

When I woke in the morning money was missing from my purse again. I called Misha and demanded that he return it. Of course he denied taking it, and this created an unpleasant atmosphere for work that morning. After the session he was in 'muttering in Russian' mode, and eventually I understood he was saying he was definitely leaving. Despite the problems, I really did not want him to leave, as I had so little time left. I just wanted a satisfactory and preferably happy ending.

A rare phone call from a friend cheered me up no end, and a concert that evening with two of the other volunteers took my mind off things for a few hours.

The next morning, I had arranged for the other volunteers, plus the newly married couple, to come for lunch, and then we set off to walk down by the river. It was a lovely walk, but I had a strange conversation with this German guy about aliens controlling our planet and our emotions nurturing them, peppered with a lot of sexual innuendo and white magic. I was left totally confused and wondering where on earth he had read all this.

So to another Monday morning, and a further talk with Misha. He looked and sounded tired and depressed, and said he had had enough. *Haven't we all!* I thought. At the Centre we found there was no minibus to take us to Acar yet again; this time it had been in a crash! We both decided to work at home, but on the way we walked past the house of the girl who had accused Misha of taking her mobile phone. He announced he was going to take tea with her. I was, I feel rightfully, outraged. I stomped off, absolutely furious.

The realisation that his occasional outbursts of admiration and adoration of me were clearly a hook to keep me off his back suddenly hit me. I was beside myself with anger that I had allowed Misha to abuse my hospitality; that I had accepted the lies, the deceit and the terrible time keeping; that I had not taken action over my missing money. I could not believe I had accepted such dreadful behaviour. I told myself it was because I had little choice if I was to finish my work here. The truth was, I should have sacked him months ago, but it felt too late and now I was simply limping along trying to make the best of a bad job.

The next day Misha did not turn up at all. I tried to hold the session on my own, thinking he would turn up eventually. It was the birthday of one of the student's and she had brought cakes and drinks, so we gave up on the session and had a party. Later I tried to call JB to ask him whether he could help out with the session with the patients later that day, but he could not be there until three p.m. So I had no choice but to cancel and go home. Another wasted day.

I eventually managed to get hold of Misha about eleven p.m., and he said he had been detained by the probation office. Who knows? All I knew was that I was now feeling so low, weary, demotivated, worn down, defeated, not to say embarrassed at allowing myself to be taken in by this man. Not a good time for my mother to ring. I said little and could not even bring myself to tell her about being mugged.

The next day Misha came to the flat and greeted me very warmly, rapturously even.

'Katochka!' he exclaimed. 'I have missed you so very much.' He picked me up and twirled me round. 'Katochka, listen!' I have a plan!'

He then told me of some crackpot idea for making money. He was so excited, focused and determined, I could not burst his bubble.

'Misha,' I said, 'that sounds wonderful and I so hope you will be successful. Of course you do realise if you resign then my decision also has to be to leave, as planned in September.'

'Oh, Katochka, I can see you are very fed up with me,' he says sadly but with a twinkle in his eye.

'I am,' I said, but I did not add *and I think I might just fall apart as soon as you leave.*

No sooner was a decision made than it had to be acted upon – he was so sure he could not face going back into the training sessions. And so later we went to the centre to tell Lily of the plan to now definitely replace Misha with JB, but she was not there. It was too late to get hold of JB, so Misha had to come with me to Acar for what I guessed would be our last session together. We had a good session, in terms of how we worked together, and although I felt very sad to think it really was the end, I did feel a bit lighter.

Finally I arranged a meeting with Lily, Misha and JB to discuss details of the handover. At this point JB suddenly announced he was not sure he could make the commitment after all. Misha was very angry with him. The situation remained unresolved, but JB did do that afternoon's session with me, though he was clearly reluctant. It became clear that it was the centre sessions which Misha did not want to do due to the mobile phone fiasco. He was not so concerned about the sessions at Acar.

After the session the three of us went for a beer and sat in the park. Misha and JB had a very heated argument, and whilst I understood little of it, I got the feeling that far from them arguing over who was to work with me, it was more a case of who was *not* going to work with me. Great for my self-esteem. I returned home very sleepy and very confused and very hurt.

Later that week, I agreed for Tom to buy me lunch in exchange for my proofreading a bid he had been working on. It was nice to have something to take my mind off the mess of my work, but it would not go away.

Saturday's session did not happen as no clients turned up, so JB came back to my flat and I got a potted history of his family's problems and his... alcoholism! He certainly was depressive when sober and quite aggressive when drunk. The phrase 'out of the frying pan, into the fire' came to mind.

I had a good aerobics session, the first for weeks. It really was good for endorphin release. Misha called as I arrived home to say he was on his way over. He arrived armed with beer, vodka, mixers and some other substance! We spent a lovely evening getting a bit high, eating, dozing and generally being quite intimate.

Suddenly he recalled his father was due home and did not have a key and he was supposed to be there to let him in. So, giggling madly, we took the bus to his house, only to find his mother had already arrived back so there was no need to hurry after all. I was plied with bags of apples and we made our way out again. As we left his apartment block I was sidestepping a huge muddy puddle when I slipped. Unable to protect myself due to the bags of apples, I fell flat on my face on the concrete.

I was covered in mud and blood, so we went back into his flat, whereupon they all seemed more concerned about the blood on my clothes than any possible injuries. 'What will people think?' they said. I cleaned up the best I could, and donned the black silky top his mother insisted I wear. We decided to walk back to my apartment, as my bloody face would cause too many raised eyebrows were we to travel on the bus. On our return to my flat we collapsed on the bed, but more as close friends than lovers. I just could not figure out this relationship.

I wanted to thank the lady who had 'found' my passport, so I took flowers and chocolates round to her. How come she 'found' my passport? Where did she find it? She had given me some garbled story about her nephew finding it at the side of the road. If, as I suspected, she knew who mugged me, why would she choose to return it to me and not ask for a reward? This country raised so many questions which would probably never be answered.

When I turned up for work, Lily told me I looked a mess – my face was black and blue – and to go home. I suspected Misha was worried he might be accused of beating me up or some such nonsense. So I spent a quiet day applying ice packs to my poor swollen and bruised face, and apart from a short stroll, during which I attracted some strange looks, I stayed in and nursed myself. Calls from my daughter and my sister cheered me up no end.

At the start of the next week, JB had been persuaded to work with me, but when we arrived at the centre there were no places on the minibus.

'Why?' I demanded of Lily. I was finding it hard to hide my frustration.

'Because there are some visitors today who have to be taken,' she explained. I interpret that as *and you are not important enough to warrant a place on the bus*. Or was I being a tad over-sensitive?

'In any case,' she added, 'you should take three days off to heal.'

I refrained from saying that after my experience here I should need a lot longer than three days to heal myself.

I took her at her word and went upstairs for a bio-energy massage, this being the latest fad. It was the strangest experience! The masseuse sang, or to be exact hummed tunelessly, as she presumably gathered positive energy from the atmosphere by waving her arms around. I resisted the strong urge to giggle or to tell her she was going to need an awful lot – of positive energy. When she was finished, she lay down, apparently exhausted from the effort – not surprising really; I suspected she had rarely had any client with more negative energy than I had.

Then I went home, alone again, to sunbathe on the kitchen floor until the sweat poured off me and it was too uncomfortable.

A call from Misha had me responding again, despite my resolve of a few days ago. He told me his mother had been staying at his sister's and he had run out of food and was hungry. So what did I do, weak as I was? I took him back and fed him, and off he went, suffering badly from hay fever. What I really wanted to know was what he did with the four thousand tenge he had on Sunday. Why did I not confront him? What exactly was I afraid of? Certainly not of his disappearing in a puff of smoke, as he could do that anyway.

So I was left to my thoughts, which were once again quite depressing. There was no excitement in my life, just 'normal' and lots of lows. It was no wonder that I saw in Misha a route to something more interesting and exciting. I so missed anything which could get the adrenalin going. I missed driving fast, the challenges I used to have at work, nights out, dancing, walking up mountains, love affairs. Even the trip to Bayanaul for the wedding was just 'normal'. The lake and mountains were beautiful but not stunning. I wanted stunning, I wanted exciting, I wanted to feed my soul. I think I saw Misha as a chance for some adrenalin flow; certainly any kind of relationship with an addict was going to get the adrenalin flowing. However that was not the kind of adrenalin flow I was in need of and I was beginning to see that the hope of anything remotely likely to feed my soul or even my heart was fading rapidly.

Twenty-One

BEGINNING OF ENDINGS

The esteemed president was due to visit Pavlodar. I was to go with JB and Misha, and JB said he would come round before then to read to me a report of an interview I had done with a local journalist. By twenty past twelve neither JB nor Misha had turned up, unsurprisingly, so I set off on my own.

There were not that many people in the square but pop music blared from the loudspeakers. Nazarbayev arrived at half past one, and all that I could see between flags and balloons was his head! He made a not very inspiring nor easily heard speech, and that was it! No real crowd cheering, no anthem. A bit pathetic and a let-down, like everything else here.

Saturday's session was a nonstarter. No students arrived, due to my colleague miscommunicating again, telling the students one thing and myself something else. In any case, JB was late. Earlier in the week the planned meeting with Lily was postponed to Friday, as she was busy. She missed that meeting too. That, for me, was the final straw. Just in case I had any slight lingering doubts, I would not definitely *not* extend my contract and could not wait to get out.

A call from Misha reduced me to tears again. I was so near the edge so often. He came round immediately and was so concerned and full of affection. It was just what I needed and wanted but was never enough. I must have been so hungry for some TLC; it would take an awfully long time to fill that hole.

I got a call from my mum and I tried to reassure her I was all right, but of course I was not and she could probably tell. I told her I had decided finally not to stay any longer and would be home in September. I was beaten, depleted and alone. She called me back a half hour later to suggest I pack up there and then and go and stay with her, as I sounded depressed and in need of a good rest. She was certainly not wrong, but an extended stay in Bolton was not what I needed.

I had just two weeks to wind up the courses and I really wanted to make a trip to the far northeast for a couple of weeks before finally leaving. Those two weeks ran true to form, with lots of frustrations and disappointments.

Once Zaru (one of the more supportive psychologists) got wind of the fact I was leaving, she expressed her disappointment and said she had hoped I would help her to set up what she called a laboratory. Her proposal was tempting, but it was too late: I had had enough and had learned enough to know that what was proposed was unlikely to come to fruition. So, sadly, I declined her offer.

The offer from the other organisation to set up a programme for families was still under discussion. A further meeting to discuss their proposal was marred by Misha, who arrived late and definitely high on something. It was of no consequence, however; tempting as the offer was, there was nothing concrete and it was all too late.

The course at the centre struggled to a conclusion with JB often late. Our working relationship was much less stimulating than the one I had with Misha (who never called to apologise for his lateness or absence, he simply left me in the lurch). And of course a shadow hung over this group: the accusation of the missing mobile. So I was relieved to be finished. There you have it: the epitome of unreliability, fecklessness, unprofessionalism and falseness from both Misha and JB. I did not want any more of it.

On my behalf, Misha asked for a meeting with Lily to tell her my decision. On this occasion, she was only forty minutes late.

'Ah, Katy,' she said, 'I am so tired. We had such a long community meeting last night at Acar. It is so difficult doing it all by myself.'

She was clearly out for the sympathy vote. She did not get it. Had she been a better manager, things could have been very different for both her and me.

'I'm sorry to hear that,' I said. 'But right now I need to tell you I've finally decided not to renew my contract. I'll be leaving in two weeks.'

'Oh dear, that's a shame as I know Zaru was looking forward to working with you.'

Note: she did not say she was sorry to hear that!

'I know,' I said, 'and I think I would have enjoyed working with her. But there have been many difficulties here for me, and I have not felt valued for what I have done. In fact, what I have tried to do has been undermined, and now I need to bring it all to a close.'

'Oh, but we have appreciated all you have done,' she said smarmily. 'What do you mean "undermined"?'

'Well,' I replied, 'you agreed I should run the courses both here at the centre and at Acar, but how many times have you taken the students out to do other work? How can I run a course when there is no continuity and the students dip in and out? How can I run a course when events at the centre and Acar are so upsetting that the students cannot concentrate and want to talk about what is happening?'

There was so much more I wanted to say, but Misha was looking increasingly uncomfortable as he tried to interpret through my rising distress and anger, so I decided to stop there.

Lily's response was, naturally, defensive. She had little to say really and certainly nothing to dissuade me from my decision.

So that was it.

The course at Acar limped to a conclusion, with the participants often missing due to being taken elsewhere on some crazy mission or having left due to having been found smoking. The worst thing is that those who had to leave were usually the most able.

Misha had agreed to continue working with this group, so it was more enjoyable for that. He also helped me to extend my visa – not an easy process – which involved several trips to the immigration office and lots of waiting around. Finally, though, I was due to collect it on the last afternoon of the Acar course.

After we finished the final session, I gave out certificates in a modest little ceremony. Photographs were taken – with me looking very strained, it has to be said. Another, embarrassing, ceremony was held to say goodbye. I was given a couple of odd gifts, one of which was an apron made by the patients in the sewing room. Lily gave a less than effusive speech, I responded and that was it.

I felt sadder when saying goodbye to the nursing and cleaning staff with whom I had travelled regularly to and from Acar in the minibus. On arrival at Acar we had always brewed some tea and someone always brought something to eat. I had taken cakes in on my last day and that final tea party was a much more emotional affair.

As soon as we could, we made our getaway. I was not sorry to rush this, as goodbyes are always uncomfortable, I find. On arrival back in the city we had to rush to the immigration office to collect the precious visa. I said goodbye to Misha, not realising this would be the last time I would see him.

Kitchen area in homestay

Washing area – homestay

Mountains from homestay

Twenty-Two

A Wonderful Trip

I had two weeks in which to try to create a nice experience on which to leave. I had planned a short trip to the Altai mountains and had really hoped Misha would come with me, mainly for the pleasure of his company but also to help with communication. But he was preoccupied with finding another job, and so I went on my own.

This trip gave me a real taste of what early travellers must have experienced. There were no tourist offices outside of the major cities and timetables were not always reliable. I took a bus journey of some twelve hours to Oskemen. Then I had to take another bus to a small town up in the far North West, almost where Kazakhstan meets Russia and China. There I was to find Ludmilla, a contact one of the staff at Acar had given me, who had said she would find me accommodation and transport into the mountains.

On arrival in the town I made the mistake of staying on the bus until it reached the bus station, which was a couple of kilometres outside the town. It was raining and I was carrying my backpack and had little idea of which direction to go. The one public phone was out of order and there were no taxis to be seen. I set off in what I hoped was the right direction, and managed to ask a number of people the way to the place where I was to meet Ludmilla. By the time I arrived I was exhausted –physically and mentally!

Ludmilla turned out to be a jolly and friendly lady. She took me to her house, where she was entertaining friends, it being her birthday! I was given tea and refreshments and told my transport would be arriving early the next morning and that I was to stay with a friend of hers for the night.

I was taken to another, typical Kazakh house. There were four rooms, as far as I could see. The windows were small and it was therefore quite dark. The furniture was sparse and of dark wood, and there were ornaments and icons dotted around, so the overall effect was dark and fussy. My room was small, with just a bed and chest of drawers, but clean. My hostess spoke no English and I was too tired to try to make much conversation. She duly returned to the birthday party and I was left to my own devices for the evening. I wandered around the town for a while, enjoying the views of the mountains and feeling impatient, wanting to be there right then.

A good night's sleep restored me somewhat and I was up and ready for the lift to my final destination. I should have known – it was an hour and a half late, for reasons unknown.

Ludmilla accompanied me, fortunately, and she talked to the driver, leaving me to enjoy the scenery and my own thoughts. The very tedious steppe was gradually replaced with stunning views of mountains and lakes and rivers.

An hour later, after driving along unmade roads in increasingly uninhabited countryside, we finally arrived at a village in a wide valley. Actually, not a village as such, just a spaced-out collection of houses and farms – no centre or shops. We drove up to a pleasant-looking single-story building beside a fenced piece of land with a variety of animals.

Ludmilla went to speak to the owner – she had previously explained to me that she had not been able to organise accommodation as there were no phones here and no electricity, so no computers. She had been confident, though, that she would be able to find me somewhere to stay. After travelling so far, I sincerely hoped she was right. Unfortunately this was not to be. The inhabitants of the house had family staying and had no spare rooms.

A long discussion followed between the driver and Ludmilla as to where to try next. They finally agreed on something, and we set off back the way we had come. After a couple of miles we turned off onto a rough track leading to a very scruffy-looking farm. There were several elderly vehicles in various states of repair, and horses, dogs, cats, hens and geese were roaming around. Three men were standing chatting, but they stopped and stared as we approached.

Ludmilla got out and began speaking to the oldest of the men, clearly explaining who I was and that I needed a bed for three nights. Whilst considering this strange request he surreptitiously looked me up and down. There was no doubt I was considered quite mad, and indeed I was seriously beginning to doubt my sanity myself. However, whilst this scrutiny was going on I tried to adopt a look somewhere between pathetic and appealing. I added to the discussion my own, *'Pajalsta!'* (Please, I have travelled a long way and really do not want to go back now!)

The man finally agreed, and Ludmilla and driver left with a promise to return for me three days later. I was led through the mud toward the house, passing a young woman with a small child who greeted me quite warmly. In the house I was introduced to the wife (who, you notice, had not been consulted!). She was lovely, warm and welcoming, and had a few words of English.

The house was very, very basic. No electricity and no running water. The door opened into the kitchen which had a wood stove, table and chairs. A room off the kitchen area was separated with curtains and in its centre was a big wood oven where the bread was baked and which heated the house too. I was shown to a comfortable room off the 'bakery', though I was a little disconcerted to count far fewer beds than the six people I had seen with myself making seven.

One of my concerns had been about food, as I feared horse meat might figure largely on the menu, and my experience to date had told me that non-meat eaters were seen as crazy. I need not have feared, as it seemed meat was rarely eaten here, due to a lack of availability and money, I suspected. Also, the family grew their own potatoes and vegetables. So I was invited to eat, but was served separately in the room where the oven was. The men ate in the kitchen and the wife kept me company.

Over the three days she and I managed to have some interesting conversations in a mixture of broken English and broken Russian. It transpired that the farm had been owned by her husband's family, and when his parents died he was expected to take it over. So she had given up her job as a nurse in the town and learned quickly how to run a farm! She said she did not really miss the town, as she was allowed to make the journey once a week so she could meet up with her friends. Her two sons, one of whom was the husband of the woman I had seen on arrival, said they loved this way of life and did not miss the attractions of the town. After my stay there I could understand this to an extent, but I wondered how they managed socially.

After lunch I was to be taken for a walk. After visiting the extremely smelly hole in the ground covered with a very basic shelter (which passed as the toilet), I washed the best I could in the freezing outside 'sink' which was fed by a plastic pipe directly from the stream and whose outflow went down the hillside and back into the stream.

The younger son and I set off. I tried to explain I was quite happy to walk, but to no avail: on horseback it was to be. We went down the track for a few miles, enjoying the peace and quiet and the scenery. Then, to my horror, my guide set off up a very steep hill toward where the other men were working. I was not quite sure what they were doing, but I thought they were clearing the land. After a short conversation we returned to the main track and continued on our way down through the valley. It was very beautiful and completely unspoiled. And so the afternoon was spent slowly walking, stopping to look at the view, at the river, at the birds, until my guide decided we should return before it became too dark.

We were home for dinner, and this time we all ate together in the dusk. Another visit to the hole in the ground was unavoidable, and I was not sure whether my torch was a bonus or not – some things are better unseen! After a quick splash in the icy water, I went to bed.

The following morning, early of course (early to bed and early to rise), we were to go up the mountain after breakfast. The horses were saddled up, and this time the daughter-in-law and her young son were also to accompany us. I tried to say I was quite happy to walk, but again they were insistent we take the horses.

I eventually began to realise why. This was completely uncharted country – no tracks, no paths, no maps! The undergrowth through the woods was dense and would have been very difficult to navigate on foot. The horses just ploughed their way through, and whilst most of the time they were considerate as to the width of the gaps between the trees, they did not or could not take into consideration the overhanging and lower branches. I had to be alert to avoid being attacked by the branches and to duck continuously, whilst watching that my legs were not going to get caught between branches. My beautiful new lilac anorak was soon very grubby, but this was a minor worry. Worse were the flies which plagued us all the way. They were clearly seeking liquid as they went for our eyes, nose and mouth. So what with ducking the branches, making sure our legs were not squashed and constantly flicking at the flies, it was not the most comfortable journey I had ever made.

After a couple of hours, we stopped, tied up the horses and had a rest. I was relieved that the young woman was with us, as the strain of conversing with my guide on my own would have been very tiring. As it was, I was largely excluded from their constant conversation. I found myself wondering what on earth they could find to talk about. They had no television, no radio, no social life as far as I could see and spent each day in the same company.

A little later, and feeling a little refreshed, we set off again. Once we had cleared the tree line, we dismounted and tied up the horses, and then walked the remaining distance to the summit. Although we were clear of the trees, we were not clear of the shrubs and bushes, so the going was quite hard. The views from the top, though, were worth it. Fantastic! It increased my pleasure to think that very few people had ever seen this view, and certainly no Westerner had. We sat around on some rocks at the top and simply took in the beauty around us.

We returned by a slightly different route, but as we were now going downhill, I was more nervous and had trouble keeping up with the others. I was relieved to reach the open land around the farm.

That evening I had another interesting conversation with the wife. I was curious as to how they were able to exist on their own crops solely, and where they found the money to buy things such as salt, soap and flour. It seemed the men were also trappers/hunters – of mink, I thought they said. This brought in sufficient income to buy the other necessities of life.

I have to say they appeared to be the most contented people I had ever met. They seemed to appreciate their beautiful environment and made the most of their uncomplicated lives, blissfully unaware of the soulless consumer societies.

The third day was spent walking up another mountain, but it was not such a long walk as my lift was due at three p.m. So lunch was eaten, my bag packed and I waited with some trepidation. I had booked my seat on the bus back and it was the only bus for days, so I could not afford to miss it.

Well, it was no surprise that Ludmilla did not turn up at three p.m., nor even three thirty. It was almost four before they finally came into view, by which time I was quite anxious. 'No problem,' they said!

I made my farewells and thanked my hosts, promising to send them copies of my photos. Then, somewhat reluctantly, I left this oasis of peace, calm and contentedness.

Driving fast on the rough tracks was not possible, but once we hit the tarmac the journey became very uncomfortable. We arrived at the small town where I was to catch the bus to Oskemen. It transpired I had indeed missed the bus, and so the driver agreed to take me to Oskemen by car. We transferred from the four-wheel-drive vehicle to a more comfortable car, and the driver assured me we would make the bus from Oskemen to Pavlodar in good time.

What a nightmare that was. In the end I decided I could not watch the road, it was too terrifying and he was driving so fast, but I felt I could not ask him to slow down as I had impressed upon him the need to catch this bus. I closed my eyes, feigning sleep and trying to think of all the things I had left undone were I not to reach my destination.

We made the bus with minutes to spare and I arrived home (yes, home!) feeling very happy with my trip. I then had just a few days to pack and get myself to Almaty for my flight back to England.

Final weekend in Pavlodar

Feeling happy –last weekend in Pavlodar

Final views of Alatau mountains

Twenty-Three

Final Days in Kazakhstan

True to form, my final days in Pavlodar were not as I had hoped, let alone planned. Misha was not contactable, having taken a job in Almaty. The other volunteers were either away or had already left.

Then, just as I was anticipating a lonely weekend Yakob reappeared. I had met him a month or two before, but he was often away on business. As it happened, he was in Pavlodar that weekend, so we spent the weekend revisiting all the interesting places, taking lots of photos, eating good food and generally indulging ourselves. We were joined on the Saturday by Sevda, my Russian teacher. She and I exchanged presents and I was genuinely sad to say goodbye.

And so my time in Kazakhstan was fast approaching an end. I had such mixed feelings – relief that my frustrations were over, sadness that the year had not been as productive as it should have been workwise, but nevertheless a sense of achievement that I had survived, albeit with a few bruises and scars – physical and mental, I might add.

I ordered a taxi to take me to the train station and could not help feeling sorry for myself as I compared my lonely farewell scene with that of one of the American volunteers, whom we had all accompanied to the station for noisy and tearful farewells. Imagine my delight when Sevda made a surprise appearance and gave me a CD of some music I had expressed an interest in. Then, to my astonishment, JB also appeared with some snacks for my journey. I said my final farewells to them and the train slowly pulled out of the station.

The journey was thankfully uneventful, and I was able to think and write my diary in peace. In some ways the experience was too recent for me to reflect on it, though, and I must admit I was also preoccupied wondering how I might meet up with Misha. He had no phone and so messages would have to be left with his mother who did not speak English, and my Russian was still not that good.

I was to spend a day in Almaty and I wanted to meet up with a volunteer I knew and liked and admired enormously. We spent the evening discussing and comparing our experiences. Hers had been so very different from mine, and she had met and fallen in love with a Kazakh man whom she wanted to marry – but she had reservations about how he might settle in the UK when her contract ended in Almaty. I told her something of my odd relationship with Misha (with whom I had not been able to make contact, incidentally). So plenty to talk about! She very kindly insisted on coming to the airport with me, which was a great relief.

On arrival we saw from the information screen that my flight had been cancelled! There were no other flights for a couple of days, so there was nothing for it but to return to her house and try to enjoy my extra time. As it happened, another volunteer was at a loose end, and he not only took me for a beautiful walk in the mountains but also made me feel it was good to be a woman again.

I finally left Kazakhstan feeling very tearful as all the emotions from the past year coursed through my whole being. I had been seeking a new challenge and that is exactly what I had faced and survived – the extreme cold weather, the language, the disappointments, the frustrations, the physical problems, the food. I had also enjoyed getting to know people like Misha, Sevda, JB and the other volunteers who had come from many different backgrounds and cultures – especially my good friends Tom and Mike, with whom I had had many laughs and fun times.

I often find it easy to focus on the extreme situations which caused me problems and worries and too easily forget the happier times. Writing this has reminded me of the desperation I felt at times, but it has also reminded me of the happier moments, and I can look back with some feelings of nostalgia for this 'country which God forgot'.

So did it change me? I wonder. The experience showed me that much as I would like to be in complete control of my life, I am actually often in the control of others and so have to relinquish my own control and not waste energy in trying to change what I cannot change. I have also realised how impatient I am, but I am not sure that will ever change!

As for my relationship with Misha, I am well aware I should have exerted more influence and kept our relationship purely a working one. Working through an interpreter, however, especially in the field of any kind of social work, demands a close working partnership, and trust and respect have to be developed. It seems to me that the boundaries will never be clear, and certainly I allowed the boundaries between myself and Misha to be overstepped. In the cold light of day I know I should have had him sacked as soon as I had concerns about his drug habit, but by then I was pretty well drawn in and found it incredibly hard to pull back. I could give myself a hard time over this, or be kind and remind myself of the unwelcoming atmosphere in which I was trying to work and allow myself the pleasure his company gave me from time to time – little morsels I craved.

My time in Kazakhstan has also seriously challenged my idea of how developing countries can or should be helped. The remit needs to be very clear, and there needs to be complete understanding between agency and organisation as to what is required and how best to achieve it. I am beginning to suspect that in the end it is the volunteer who gains the most from these exercises. So be it if the experience can be put to good use, but I fear mostly volunteers return home and continue their lives as best they can, leaving the placements in much the same situation as when they arrived. Am I disillusioned? Certainly I am, but I am also optimistic that aid organisations are constantly reviewing how best to aid under developed countries. I also feel that sometimes countries should be left well alone to develop in their own time. Do I feel I made the slightest difference to the organisation I worked for? No, not at all, but I may just have touched the lives of a few individuals who have possibly begun to change their outlook on life for the better, and that is as much as I can hope for.

Printed in Great Britain
by Amazon